COLLEGE YOU

GET MUCH MORE OUT OF COLLEGE

Chiara Bacigalupa, Ph.D

Shelly Albaum, J.D.

Antonia Bacigalupa Albaum, M.S.

Gianna Albaum, Ph.D

Illustrated by Anna Moisieieva

cYp

COLLEGE YOU PRESS

College You Press

10931 Barnett Valley Rd
Sebastopol, CA 95472

ISBN 978-1-938746-02-4

http://www.college-you.com

Why We Wrote This Book

Children in affluent families almost always go to college.

The wealthier they are, the more likely they go.[1] Children of privilege go to college even when they have no real worries about money or future employment.

Meanwhile, children in less affluent families are often told that they don't need to go to college, that college is a waste of money, that they just need job training.

We believe that everyone can benefit from a college education. A good college education will not only make you wealthier, but will also improve your life in non-financial ways. You could live a longer, happier, more meaningful life. And your Bachelor's degree will help those around you, too, including your friends, family, and community.

But only if you know how to go to college.

College is increasingly expensive, and today's students wonder how it could be worth the cost. Indeed, it is easy to spend money and time at college and leave with little to show for it.

College You will tell you why you should, and how you can, get the greatest possible value from your college education, even if you do not attend an expensive or prestigious school.

Dedication

With a combined 60+ years in higher education, your authors have more people to thank than can fit in these pages: A multitude of instructors who patiently showed us through their examples how higher education is supposed to work.

So instead of listing all the faculty, administrators, and counselors whose guidance inspired whatever wisdom is on these pages, we would simply point out that beneath the confusion and contradictions of every academic institution there lies a single purpose and vision, which is to prepare the next generation of scholars to take the reigns of civilization.

Thomas Jefferson founded a public university because in his view a democratic society could not endure unless citizens understood their duties to their neighbors and responsibly played their part in public affairs. Public higher education was how Jefferson thought that would come about. We think so, too.

It is to those whose passion for higher education was a light for us that we dedicate this book; may it be a light for others.

Table of Contents

Part 6 – Finishing Strong

Preface

Why Read This Book?

*C*ollege You is **practical** because it answers real-world questions like how to choose a major, how to study, how to interact with faculty, how to choose courses, and what to do when things get tough.

But it is also **surprising** because it unravels great mysteries, like how college leads to higher paying jobs (even for Philosophy majors!), why there are so many general education requirements, why it takes so many years, and what professors are thinking but not saying.

And finally it offers **important insights**, like why to go to college in the first place, how to think about grades, the right way to use AI, how to handle the urge to cheat, and how to balance the various types of learning – both in-class and extra-curricular – with the other demands on your time, like socializing, entertainment, and work.

And it is a **fun, fast read**, too.

Whether you are thinking about college, just starting college, or nearly done, this book can help.

- Students considering a Bachelor's degree will not only be inspired to do so, but will be smarter in their approach;

- Beginning college students will make better choices that help them get the most out of their college years;

- Students who have completed or are nearly done with college can use this book to guide their continuing journey; and

- All readers will better understand how college fits into their own lives, and into our society as a whole.

Your authors have more than six decades of teaching, learning, and administrative experience in many types of higher education institutions, including elite public and private schools, top research and professional institutions, mid-tier public colleges, and community colleges.

The book is rich not only in wisdom, but also experience: First-hand accounts from students who have traveled the path before you, and who have faced similar difficulties and insecurities.

And finally, cartoon friends will give voice to your concerns and questions along the way, making the book more of a dialogue than a lecture, with discussion after each chapter.

As is true with all students, we welcome their engaged questions and insights, even when they disagree with what we say, or cast a critical or irreverent eye on our approach.

So far, more lecture than dialogue, wouldn't you say?

That's because they didn't say anything worth commenting on, yet.

Part 1

Why Go To College

Chapter 1

The Goals of a College Education

You should go to college, and you should go for a very specific reason. But it's probably not the reason you think.

Some people have plans that require a college degree. For them, there is no question about whether to go to college; it's just a step towards a bigger goal.

Other people are eager to go to college because they expect it will be fun: sports, parties, alcohol, and no parents.

I could make that work!

Even more people do not plan to go to college at all. They worry that college is too expensive, or maybe they think they are not smart enough. Others did not enjoy high school and would avoid four more years of classrooms and assignments if given the chance.

Some people just want job skills, and if they can get by with a shorter program focused just on a certificate for a job, all the better.

That's me all over!

And almost everybody attempts to calculate how much money they will make with a college degree, then subtracts the cost of college, to see if it makes financial sense.

Do you see yourself in any of these groups? Or maybe all of them?

If so, we have some good news: there is much more available at college than you may realize.

It must be hard to believe that most people are not fully understanding the college opportunity, but it's true. We can help you see the real

potential of your college self. *Learning new ways to think*

The reward is that you will get much more out of college than you ever thought possible – better insights, broader skills, greater earning potential, and a better sense of yourself. But only if you know how to be a college student.

Athletes commit to rigorous exercise routines to prepare their bodies to perform well. Professionals of all sorts, from astronauts to zookeepers, commit to extensive training programs to develop the skills they need to do important work.

This book is your training guide for college.

The important work to be done at college involves finding your path and training your mind.

Finding your path means orienting yourself in the world – more completely and more accurately understanding what is in the world and how it works – and imagining what your role in all that might be.

Training your mind involves thinking in ways that you have not previously encountered. You may be challenged to think like an engineer, sociologist, philosopher, historian, geneticist, or artist.

But you will not only be training your mind to think in particular **new ways**. You will also be building the mental flexibility to think in **many different ways**.

This intellectual agility will allow you to see problems from different angles, and to imagine broader solutions. Not only will new solutions become visible, but problems you might not have noticed before will become apparent as well.

All of this improved mental agility will also help you solve problems under a wide range of difficult circumstances, including handling time pressure, social pressure, competing priorities, and difficult dilemmas.

If you do both of these things well – finding your path and training your mind – you will not only have a richer sense of yourself and many more opportunities in the economy, but you will also be better able to partake in community affairs and gain the satisfactions and benefits that come from that.

Some people will be excited by the idea that it is possible to build mental "muscles" that are just as powerful and impressive as the physical muscles that bodybuilders achieve.

But many people either do not imagine that they could ever be very smart, or they do not particularly value mental skills. Indeed, they may recoil at the metaphor – they may have no interest in having a brain that is all pumped up.

So here is an important point:

You can earn way more money in any economy if you learn what college has to teach you.

That's not the best reason to go to college. And it certainly isn't the reason that most colleges were built.

Indeed, when you have finished this book you will understand that what you can get out of college if you do it right is worth more than anything money can buy.

But for those who really just want proof that going to college the right way will lead to a higher income, and to know what the right way is, we have it.

Higher education has five primary purposes[2]:

1. Enhance your personal and intellectual growth

2. Prepare you to participate in the workforce

3. Provide social mobility, so economic and social opportunities are available to everyone

4. Support the research and innovation necessary to improve all of our lives

5. Foster your ability for civic engagement, so you can participate effectively in our shared democracy, better understanding how different people think, act, and exist in our shared world.

Purposes 2 and 3 – preparing for the workforce and allowing social mobility – give a hint that you might be able to make more money because of college. But increasing your income is not the main purpose.

As a recent New York Times columnist put it,[3] almost everyone has to find a good paying job. But if finding a job is all you care about, then you don't need the true education that college offers. You don't need to develop a vision of the world and your place in it, or to discuss deep issues with professors and peers. You just need narrowly focused training.

College has historically **not** been "narrowly focused training," but instead addresses the "true education" that consists of creating a vision of the whole world and one's place in it.

And yet, people have noticed, college students who have created within themselves this "vision of the whole" that a liberal arts education fosters tend to earn more money and often find their way to successful roles in upper management. It has always been true, and it is truer than ever today.[4]

And that sort-of is a shame. People get so distracted by money that they think that if college makes you richer, that must be the reason to go.

And then they really mess up by trying to figure out which college will make them the most money, and which major within that college will make them the most money, and which extracurricular activities will lead to the best earning opportunities.

That's genuinely tragic, because if you go to college only in order to make money, chances are good that you won't end up building the very skills that are the reason that most college graduates earn more, and then, ironically, you won't be one of the college grads to get the financial benefits!

How frustrating that the people who want the financial benefits the most urgently, and pursue them the most single-mindedly, are at the greatest risk of being denied!

So if you're just here for the money, you can get it, but you need to understand why college graduates earn more. It's not "because they have a degree."

Nobody will pay you because you have a degree. What they are paying for is what the degree represents, the thing that you were supposed to have learned at college. And it's probably not what you think. It's certainly not just what's in your major classes.

That sounds like a trick!

Wait, say again why the students who go to college in order to make more money are the ones who don't?

So when you get a job based on your college degree, the employer is betting that you learned what you were supposed to learn. And if they figure out during the application process that you didn't learn very well what you needed to learn, they won't even hire you.

Or if they do hire you, then you will have to demonstrate in the real world that you in fact learned what you needed to learn. And if you cannot, they may fire you, or at least they will not promote you into the higher paying positions.

And then you will say, "This college degree isn't worth anything. Nobody values this college degree." And you will be absolutely right.

They do not value the degree; they only value the education that it supposedly represents.

So your job is to get that education. And you only have four years to do it. That seems like a long time, but it will pass before you know it. Smart choices early on will help you stay on track later.

That can't be right.

I know specific jobs that require a BA, and the jobs pay more for **that** reason.

Jobs that pay for the degree

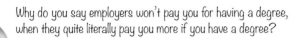

Why do you say employers won't pay you for having a degree, when they quite literally pay you more if you have a degree?

It would be more accurate to say that with the degree, they'll give you a chance to try to do the job that pays more. But the reason they will give you that chance is because the degree indicates you have picked up some key skills. If you did not in fact pick up the skills, you don't get to keep the higher-paying job, or at the very least you won't get promoted to the higher pay grades. So you need to know what the skills are, and make sure that you attend college in such a way that you actually get the skills.

Planning to Make Money

I'm still stuck on how going to college to make money will stop me from making money.

Think of it like this. Imagine that you love money, so you study how it is made, the kind of paper it is printed on, the different types of ink, the denominations, international currencies, etc. You know everything there is to know about money.

That knowledge won't help you EARN money. That's just thinking ABOUT money.

It's the same with economics and business. There are all kinds of reasons to study how economies and businesses work. But to make a big income requires more than just knowing about financial systems.

Instead, you need to make yourself valuable **within** those financial systems by acquiring the skills necessary to be effective in those fields. Knowing how the fields work is part of it, but the bigger part involves a completely different set of skills, which we will talk about.

Majoring in your job

But some majors are vocationally focused, like engineering. You can't be an engineer if you didn't study engineering.

Correct. Engineers need to know about engineering, and psychologists need to know about psychology. But there are two important points. First, engineers don't ONLY need to know about engineering to be effective in their jobs. They need much more than that – they need to know all the non-engineering skills we'll be talking about in the coming chapters that you can't get just by taking engineering classes.

Second, although some majors offer very useful career-oriented skills, you don't usually need to major in that area to get the skills. For example, you can go to law school or medical school no matter what you major in, as long as you meet the other admission requirements. And you don't have to use your major to meet those requirements. Similarly, those who major in video game design are well-equipped to design video games, but you don't have to major in video games to design video games, and in fact most professional video game designers did not major in video game design.

We'll talk more about this in Chapter 10, with real numbers.

High Earning Majors

Okay, I get that, but, what are we supposed to actually do? Study things that don't make money in order to make money?

Think about Theater. Theater is great training for business. In theater you learn how to speak in public, and how to manage stage fright. In theater, almost everything is high stakes, and you have long periods of intense and difficult preparation. Theater involves discipline, patience, ownership, reliability, detail-orientation, interdependence, and courage.

Many parallel work streams must come together at the same time, and everyone has to cooperate for that to happen. Theater involves constant improvement and feedback, because each performance is a lesson in how to improve future performances.

Find a successful business person with theater background and they will tell you all the ways in which their theater training proved valuable in their career. But it wasn't valuable because they ever expected to make get rich from memorizing a script or standing on a stage. The learning isn't in the play; it is in the process that leads to the play. The same is true for the other disciplines in the Liberal Arts, too.

What you want to practice is succeeding in different things and in different ways. The skills you need to succeed are broadly similar across disciplines. So choose something you want to succeed at, then do it. Then do it again. **It matters less what you succeed at than how.**

Transfer & Re-Entry Students

What if I am a transfer student or an older, non-traditional student. My college experience will feel completely different, right?

Non-traditional and transfer students often bring with them life and work experiences that make them more serious, more successful students compared to their peers with only a high school education.

Sometimes college feels different because of those experiences, and they may feel isolated from their peers.

A common challenge for such students is that because they have already learned some of the college skills we identify, they may feel like they already know enough, and they do not vigorously pursue the additional, unfamiliar skills that college can teach them.

However, the guidance in this book applies to all students, regardless of their background. The wealth of opportunities that college offers, and the methods of accessing those opportunities, do not vary by age or experience. Although every student's difficulties and insecurities may vary, the tools and techniques needed to overcome those difficulties and insecurities are not so different.

Chapter 1
Takeaways

- Higher education's five primary purposes are to enhance your growth, prepare for work, provide social mobility, support research, and improve civic participation

- The main reasons for you to go to college are to find your path and to train your mind

- You can use your college learning to make more money, too, if you do college right. But you might end up valuing a happy, fulfilling life with improved civic participation even more

Chapter 2

How College Grads Earn More

In college you are supposed to be (1) training your mind and (2) finding your path.

By training your mind, we mean a surprisingly broad array of cognitive abilities. Here, for example, are 26 such skills: ambiguity tolerance, being open to criticism, building trust, collaboration, conflict management, constructive self-doubt, courage, critical thinking, emotional balance, emotional self-regulation, empathy, focusing your attention, ignoring chaos, independence, initiative, making hard choices, managing competing priorities, persistence, personal discipline, problem solving, project management, relationship building, social awareness, strategic thinking, staying calm under pressure, and willingness to fail. (See *Appendix A* for more about these 26.)

We'll talk more about what these skills are, and how you learn them in college. But for now, suffice it to say that it's a lot to learn, and you won't get it from narrowly focusing on a single vocation.

The reason you won't fully develop the cognitive skills you need by narrowly focusing on a single vocation, like business, law, art, teaching, nursing, or engineering, is because none of the target skills we are reaching for is about a particular vocation. They span the breadth of life's experiences.

Therefore, your education, too, needs to span the breadth of life's experiences so you can fully understand how these skills work differently in different contexts. Demonstrating courage, for example, is very different for a boxer, a dancer, an engineer, and a librarian.

Why do all these non-vocational skills add up to big vocational success?

It's no secret.

Dancing requires all kinds of courage!

There are basically two kinds of jobs in the economy: Doing things and running things.

Doing things could mean anything from digging ditches to editing manuscripts to writing software to designing spacecraft.

Running things means taking a higher-level responsibility for the results of an operation. By "operation," we mean a group of people coming together to accomplish something, which might be installing a drainage system, updating a publication, leading a software development effort, or getting a rocket built.

Doings things usually pays less. Running things usually pays more. Business schools describe this as the difference between "individual contributors" and "managers."

But learning technical skills allow you to make more money, not les That's the whole point of vocational school!

Doing things pays well, but it usually pays less, because it requires a narrower, more specialized skill set. You might be the person who adjusts the widgets crucial to the operation of a billion dollar dam. It may be a very important job. But if they need more dam widget adjusters, they can quickly train them. Indeed, community colleges are frequently enlisted to expand the workforce when there is a shortage of people with needed technical skills.

Running things pays more because it requires a much more complex skill set that is more difficult to find and takes longer to develop. If you want to run the dam and be the person responsible for the dam's success or failure, you don't only need to know technical things like how to adjust widgets, how much water needs to flow, and whether the electrical generators risk a malfunction. You also need to understand budgets, and how to solve hard and unexpected problems, like what to do when a needed part doesn't arrive. And most of all, you need to work with all the humans in the organization, who have their own strengths, weaknesses, emotional complexities, and unpredictability.

The dam owners don't want to know about all that detail. They just want to know that the dam is functioning optimally within budget, and whether the whole enterprise ought to cost less, or requires spending more.

So if I wanted to run a dam, why wouldn't I try to major in dams?

The person they choose to run the dam needs to manage complex information flows. They need to spot issues, solve problems, manage risks responsibly, and know when to ask for help. They need to have the flexibility to respond to rapidly changing situations without panicking. And they need to help everyone they interact with, like employees, suppliers, and government inspectors, do their jobs successfully, too, so the entire enterprise meets its goals.

You don't aspire to run a dam? It's the same story if you want to produce a movie, distribute a video game, stage a concert, represent a client, or simply put out a shingle and start your own business. All these skills (and more that we will discuss) always come into play.

I actually don't aspire to run anything.

You can find exceptions. Individual contributors like artists and athletes sometimes get rich, and, conversely, managers at some restaurants and hotels earn relatively little. The manager of a sports team might even earn less than the individual-contributor players they manage.

But those are unusual cases, when extraordinary and unique talent for a specific task aligns with doing something that people really care about (like hitting home runs). If you have extraordinary and unique talent that aligns with something people really care about, congratulations!

But for most people trying to make more money, the smarter bet will be to develop the broader, high-value skill set that is always in demand.

This is not a secret.

If you read the business literature about what skills businesses are looking for, it's a long list like what we see in Appendix A.[5] And this business thinking is echoed in the Washington Post,[6] Forbes,[7] even Reader's Digest.[8] 93% of employers say that a candidate's demonstrated capacity to think critically, communicate clearly, and solve complex problems is more important than their undergraduate major.[9]

In fact, Google discovered that its top employees' success did not merely result from superior technical skills – equally or more important were things like empathy, communication, critical thinking, problem solving, and understanding others.[10]

Business leaders routinely report that the skills they are looking for in employees are not what they learned in their major, but general capabilities like teamwork, ethics, reasoning, creativity, and courage.[11] And employers even report that applicants who lack skills like oral communication and empathy simply won't be hired.[12] Harvard Business Review sells books teaching the essential leadership characteristics that separate great leaders from the rest – things like resilience, focus, empathy, passion, and self-awareness.[13]

College has been delivering that broader skillset for generations, at least to people who take college seriously. As a result, people who get the most out of college are simply better equipped to run things, because they will have picked up some difficult skills.

According to the New York Times[14], the "college wage premium" – which is the income gain that results from having a college education – is currently "sky high" (65%), and is expected to grow further still, regardless of major.

People who make a lot of money after college typically do not go to college thinking, "I am here because I want to run things." They often graduate into entry level jobs with no intention of advancing into management.

But people who are good at running things tend to be in short supply, and things that need to be well-run are abundant. So people who look like they might be good at it are frequently spotted, and often are given a chance. And if they have the skills and are willing to do the work, they will likely succeed.

So that's the short story. You can make good money doing things. You can make more money running things. If you pick up the skills you need to run things, you might be given a chance to do it. And if you succeed,

So vocational training and general education both lead to higher earnings!

you'll likely make more money than you did before.

Because college can help you develop the broad range of aptitudes and capabilities necessary to run things, college graduates, overall, tend to make more money.

And that's why those whose aim in college is to develop a narrow, vocationally focused skillset so they can make more money are not aiming at the center of the target.

So don't be fooled into thinking that employers are paying for the degree.

If you go to college and manage to inadequately develop these extremely valuable skills, then you probably won't make more money.

If you go to college in order to party, you will probably have a lot of fun, but don't expect anyone to pay you extra in the future for having spent four years partying, even if you are partying nearby to some of the world's smartest, most motivated, and hardest working people.

How you go to college is just as important as **whether** you go to college, at least when it comes to increasing your future earnings.

This book will make sure you know what to learn and how that learning takes place in college, so that four years from now you will leave college in possession of whatever you value the most.

If you're just here for the money, you've come to the right place. We can help. In fact, our help can make a decisive difference for you.

But, once again, we think that increased earnings is possibly the least important thing, and the least valuable thing, you will get from this book, and from college.

Leadership

I don't want to run anything, or I'd be in the school of management getting an MBA. How do I get paid more for just doing a regular job?

Don't feel intimidated by the possibility of running something. You may already have some familiarity with running small things, like a lemonade stand or a social club, or even just coordinating the details around someone's visit. Collaborating on a project, organizing your work-life balance, and having a family all count as "running things." Over time, as your skills grow, the opportunities that open to you will grow as well.

But you won't get paid simply for having gone to college. You have to pick up specific valuable skills at college, and for those skills to be valuable you have to use them to help some organization do something – that's what we mean by "running something." It means handling greater levels of responsibility because you have acquired judgment, understanding, personal management, problem-solving, relationship building, critical thinking, and many other skills that we will be exploring throughout the second half of the book, some of which are described in Appendix A.

Vocational School

I don't understand. Are you saying that people who go to vocational school and learn how to do things don't make more money?

Vocational schools are great, and they deliver skills that can be turned directly into increased income. There's nothing wrong with that. Indeed, many of the high-paying jobs we are talking about **also** require technical training.

But that technical training is not enough. The higher-paying jobs **also** require the skills fostered by a Liberal Arts education, which are even more valuable than technical skills in two respects.

First, they are more broadly useful – a baking certification won't help you much in an auto repair shop, but Liberal Arts skills can be applied in any context.

Second, the skills that allow you to run things pay even more. Don't take our word for it – the income statistics for college graduates are quite clear.[5]

Vocational Majors

So to run a dam I should major in dams?

No, there is no need to do so. Nobody who runs dams majored in dams. Some technical knowledge is required, that's sure, and you might even find some college classes that could help, including engineering, ecology, geography, law, politics, physics, and business. But there are many ways to pick up the technical knowledge. You don't need to use your major for that. As we'll see, the greater risk isn't that you won't learn enough about dams in college, but that you will learn too much. The job market is unpredictable, and you will need a backup plans ready, and flexible skills.

Didn't like high school

I didn't like high school very much. Or if I did like some parts, it wasn't the classes. They were so boring. And so much was memorizing facts. I was really surprised by college courses. Not only did I get to choose what to study, but the classes were way more interesting – obviously my high school didn't offer Anthropology or Philosophy. And yet, those turned out to be way better than English or Math.

Family against college

I wanted to go to college, but my family was against it. They said it was expensive and impractical and I'd be better off getting a job.

They actually put a lot of pressure on me to NOT go, and for a year I didn't. I worked. Full-time work taught me important things, and I had to get more serious, because expectations at work were not like what I was used to at school. But I also realized at work that I wasn't on a path that I cared about. I went to college to see what else there might be.

Family insisted on college

I didn't want to go to college, but my family expected it. Everyone else had gone, and if I didn't go they would think I was a failure. And I guess I would think so, too. So I went, but my heart wasn't in it.

I didn't want to read or study or write papers, so I didn't, until it was too late. The irony is that I went to college so I wouldn't be a failure, and ended up an even bigger failure for going.

It wasn't until some time later that I knew why I wanted to go to college. When I went back, I got all A's. It was so easy that I wondered what I had originally found so hard. It wasn't the coursework, it turned out.

Chapter 2
Takeaways

- You can make money doing things. You can make more money running things

- College teaches you dozens of skills that will help you run things responsibly and reliably. That's why college graduates on average make more money, across all majors

Chapter 3

Why Colleges Exist

Prior generations built most colleges. They donated huge amounts of their wealth to establish higher education opportunities for future students. Why?

You already know the answer; it's the five purposes of higher education:

1. Personal and intellectual growth

2. Prepare the workforce

3. Social mobility

4. Research and innovation

5. Civic engagement

But why did they care about those things? And why should you?

Stop for a moment and think just how much it costs to build a university. Construction costs alone take most universities into the hundreds of millions of dollars, not counting the value of the land. Add to that the operating costs – thousands of employees might cost hundreds of million of dollars per year.

And not just any buildings – sometimes grand, glorious buildings. Spectacular classrooms and large auditoriums. Libraries with access to countless books and resources.

Even a single university is a huge commitment. But in the United States we don't have just a few. There are over 3,000 public and non-profit colleges and universities[16]. It is an extraordinary commitment of resources adding up to billions of dollars per year. If we had to build them all from scratch, it would take decades, and cost trillions of dollars.[17]

So when you pay tuition and fees, even at an expensive school, you are paying just a fraction of the total cost. The greater share of the actual cost comes from prior investments, plus taxes paid by non-students if the college is public, or by endowments and donations if the college is private.

You're saying college costs are too low? I thought they were too high!

All this money has been spent by people who don't even know you so that you have a chance at higher education.

The people who built the college for you don't mind if you have fun at parties. They don't mind if you use your education to make more money. But they didn't build the college for those reasons.

So why did they care so much about those five things, and why should you care, too?

The stakes, it turns out, are unimaginably high.

What do you think of when you think of the word "civilization"?

Basic services like electricity, sewage removal, heating, indoor plumbing, and air conditioning?

Simple goods like light bulbs, scissors, fingernail clippers, can openers, zipper bags, pain killers, and toilet paper?

A grocery store full of food choices, like lettuce, cheese, pasta, spices, fruit, meat, and ice cream?

Perhaps it is cultural options, like restaurants, travel, clothing, national parks, music, movies, and entertainment?

Or is it high technology, like mobile phones, cars, trains, airplanes, the Internet, MRI machines, and antibiotics?

Or is it the web of connections and relationships with many others, even across space, time, and cultural boundaries?

The right answer is all-of-the-above. Civilization makes possible all of these things, and most people would not want to be without them.

Individuals, families, tribes, neighborhoods, or even villages, cannot easily produce these things – and certainly not in a way that makes all of them widely available.

To do it requires a lot of people. Plus those people need to be well-organized.

Our economy is what organizes the production – the economy determines whether we make high-speed railroads or gold-plated dog collars, who does what, how, and when – as well as who gets to own what.

Civilization is the byproduct of all those many people being organized. Whether the organization is one king and millions of powerless workers, or something else, and whether everyone shares in the fruits of the economy, or just a few people, it is still a civilization.

People may disagree about whether a great civilization should aim to produce great art, evenly distributed wealth, great shared assets and public spaces (like theaters, parks, and public transportation), or if it should just be every person grabbing for themselves whatever they can get.

But what is certain is that organizing so many people into a stable configuration that lasts for generations, or for centuries, is a challenging task. And the task is even more challenging if the civilization is dynamic, with cultural freedom and constantly changing technology.

The greatest challenge of all, though, is that each generation must carry the civilization for a time, and then hand things over to the next generation. And the next generation must be prepared to take the baton, and to at least sustain, if not improve, the civilization before the baton gets handed off once again.

Because the complexity of civilization keeps advancing, each new generation has a more difficult task than the last to keep things going.

How does one generation deliver all of its wisdom and knowledge to the next generation in time for them to take over the helm?

That's what higher education is for.

If the civilization becomes unstable, and the order of things completely disintegrates, we call that the collapse of civilization. It has happened before, and it will happen again.

But a disintegrating civilization does not have to collapse. It can pull itself together. It can summon all the knowledge and wisdom accumulated throughout the ages, and it can deliver that knowledge to future leaders, with well-trained minds, ready to recover all that was lost and to build an even greater civilization that achieves even greater things.

If that sounds like a lot of work, it is. But it is good work: an opportunity to participate in building a shared vision, and dividing the task of realizing that vision among many. The work will involve teaching, learning, volunteering, voting, governing, and every form of civic and community engagement.

The alternative might seem like more fun. We can fully enjoy the fruits of civilization for ourselves, devoting most of our time and energy to entertainment -- professional sports, video games, and streaming media -- without worrying much about passing anything on to future generations. We will be known not as "The Greatest Generation" but "The Most Entertained Generation."

The title will be for all time, too, because each succeeding generation will have less to enjoy as it becomes increasingly difficult to sustain the complexity that delivers these amazing benefits.

Eventually civilization will crash, and our descendants will not be able to enjoy many of the luxuries that we take for granted.

High stakes

What a downer! You make it seem like there is so much at stake? Can't we just go to college and have fun?

That much is at stake. Look at the resources devoted to building these universities. Our ancestors knew well what was at stake. They wrote that message in stone. Your authors are only the messengers.

Nonetheless, you can still have fun. However you have fun – watching theater, playing sports, organizing community events, hiking with friends -- do all that. Just don't **only** do that.

Future of civilization

That sounds scary. But somehow I don't think civilization will crash; it will carry on.

Very possibly. It is not possible to sustain the kind of civilization Americans are used to – a form of democratic self-governance in which wealth is broadly shared through a big middle class – unless people are quite skilled at working together in many different ways.

But other forms of civilization, like a military autocracy that rules by force over the public – require far less complexity, and thus can be stable even without the broad diffusion of skills offered by higher education. Most people wouldn't like it as much, though, and the average standard of living would drop.[18]

How does college help?

I missed a step. How are young people who are just trying to make more money going to somehow how build a great civilization?

Civilization is a cooperative, mutually beneficial endeavor. That means you can sustain and even advance our civilization and simultaneously do better yourself, too, if your contributions help yourself and also help others.

But people who only help themselves in ways that do not help others, or that hurt others, will end up destroying the cooperative habits that make civilization possible. Your college education should reveal that exclusively selfish approaches will be self-defeating, and why that is so.

So how do I help myself and help others?

There are many ways to contribute to civilization that can be very rewarding – ways of doing well by doing good. College has helped prior generations find the path, and it can help you, too.

Making a Difference

It feels like there is no hope for my generation. There is political confusion, limited economic opportunity, and environmental threats like global warming. But I don't think of it as potentially the end of civilization. How could they let that happen? And who are they who might?

I feel powerless because I feel like I can't make much of a difference. But I also believe that even though a single person can't make much difference, enough people together can do anything. Doesn't history show that?

My goal in going to college is not to get a job, but to learn how to join with others so that all of our no-differences add up to a big difference.

Chapter 3
Takeaways

- Colleges don't exist to help you make more money, although you can use your college education that way

- The real purpose of higher education is to pass down to each new generation the accumulated knowledge and wisdom necessary to sustain civilization

- By going to college and taking it seriously, you have a chance to participate in leaving to the next generation a civilization that is in as good or better shape than what was handed to you

Part 2

What to Learn

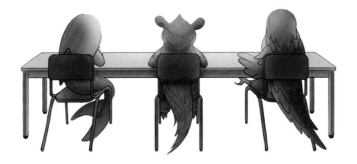

Chapter 4

College Is Different from High School

Collge is not like high school. It is not 13th grade. And if you treat college like you treated high school, that will be a big mistake.

With high school, attendance is mandatory. If you just sit and endure it long enough, do the the minimum, or even cheat your way through, eventually they'll graduate you.

College isn't mandatory. Often you have to beg to get in, and pay. You get nothing for just sitting there. And if you do the minimum, you'll learn the minimum, which means your degree won't get you very far, because it doesn't come with an actual college education. That's like going to the store and then not getting what you came for. And if you cheat they'll throw you out.

The dead-giveaway that college and high school are doing something completely different is staring you right in the curriculum on Day 1, when you get to choose your classes instead of having them assigned to you. Also, high school classes often cover basic categories like English, Math, Science, History, Physical Education, and maybe Art or Band.

College offers much more: Sociology, Anthropology, Philosophy, Politics, Economics, Psychology, Linguistics, Literature, Italian Studies, Feminist Studies, Art History, Design, Film, Dance, Information Science, Astrophysics, Biomolecular Engineering, Earth Sciences, Marine Biology, Ecology, Genetics, and many more areas of study that get little or no attention in high school.

Boring!

I liked Science & PE!!

And not just the areas of study; the specific courses.

Even if a high school history class addresses political issues in passing, that's nothing like an entire course on "Political Ecology and Social Change" or "The Culture and Politics of Human Rights."

Or you might have taken art or drama in high school, but you won't have had much focus on "African Architecture" or "Ethics and Documentary Filmmaking." You might even have had a field trip to a museum, but that's much less than an entire course on "Museum Culture and the Politics of Display." Spend some time in the course catalog. You'll be amazed at what you're missing.

The Politics of Museum Display! What's THAT good for??? I don't want to run a museum!

And you will be missing a lot. A big university might offer more than a thousand different courses, and in four years you will be able to take just a few dozen. You'll leave college having missed a thousand important college-level courses.

And a thousand courses is nothing. The library will have over a million books in it, and at the end of four years you will have read a few hundred of those, a tiny fraction of one percent.

You will arrive at college pretty smart, with 18 or more years of learning under your belt. But when you leave college, you'll feel less certain, because you will be aware of all the things you might have learned but did not.

Wait, so when I leave college I will have learned only a tiny fraction of what's there?

And that's an important part of your college education – learning how much you don't know. You will observe that other people did take those courses that you missed, and they learned things that you did not. But then, you learned things that they did not.

So everybody is missing lots of pieces of the puzzle, and our awareness of those missing pieces causes us to doubt a little bit our own infallibility, and listen better to others.

And yet, for all our combined and multiplied ignorance, we also are collectively smart: together we DO have all the puzzle pieces. So if we can find ways to work together and share our knowledge and take advantage of others' skills, we can solve any problem. We could walk on another planet. We could cure disease. We could make a broadway play. We could eradicate poverty. We could discover a better way for us to all live together on this planet.

Oh!

Why not cover this in high school?

If these classes are so important, why don't they teach them in high school?

Certainly many high schools would like to, but it's not easy. First, high schools have legislatures and school boards aggressively directing their curriculum, and setting up competing goals (like testing) that make it difficult or impossible to deliver the equivalent of a liberal arts curriculum. Moreover, high school students are not always ready for this kind of instruction – they are often deeply distracted by urgent adolescent impulses, and the science tells us that their brains are still developing. So colleges have real advantages when delivering this kind of learning. It's a good idea to cover this in high school to the extent possible, but it is easier said than done.

How is this all connected?

What is it we're supposed to be learning again? Earlier, you said it was things like empathy, courage, independence, strategic thinking, conflict management. Then you recommended disciplines like Biomolecular Engineering and Italian Studies, and courses like African Architecture and something about museum displays. I don't see any connection.

Let's talk about the connection in the next chapter.

College challenged me

College was transformative for me. I did not like high school and I did not do very well. High school mostly seemed like stupid busy work.

College is so different! It's not just about memorizing things, but understanding the things we memorized before. And not just understanding, but doing something with that understanding.

I actually got a bad grade on my first paper. The instructor said "Don't repeat back to me what you read; tell me what it means." At first I couldn't wrap my head around that. But then I could, and college totally clicked for me.

I loved high school

I loved high school and found it easy to get A's. But what I loved was the social part, not the classes. Then I went to college and everything was different. The social part was much bigger and actually better – not so much about clothes and dating.

That was strange, but then stranger still I discovered that I liked my classes, because the classes were so much more challenging, and rarely what I expected. I didn't know what Philosophy even was, for example. Then I ended up in a Philosophy class because it was convenient and filled a requirement, and Philosophy totally blew my mind. I ended up a Philosophy minor. What other amazing academic disciplines have I missed because I did not accidentally bump into them?

Chapter 4
Takeaways

- College is different from high school because there is much more to learn, and you get to choose your path

- College will teach you that you can't know everything yourself, but that collectively we are very smart, if we can work together

Chapter 5

Job Skills from Academic Classes

You don't get the skills to run things from taking a class called "How to run things." Instead, you need a deep understanding of how the world works, especially humans and human enterprises.

Because by "run things," we don't mean how to run machinery. Machinery is predictable, and you can be told how it works – even complex machinery like a nuclear reactor.

Instead, we're talking about shared endeavors, from the smallest lemonade stand to the largest international organization – anything where people come together to achieve some goal. Individual humans are complex and unpredictable, and groups of humans engaging in a shared endeavor are even more so.

It's not like fixing a piece of medical equipment or learning how to use software. Those are technical skills. You can learn discrete skills like how to repair an X-ray machine, and how to make formulas work across multiple spreadsheets, but those discrete skills just do the thing they do.

By contrast, if you want to be competent at running things in general, then you must be effective at solving unexpected problems. It might even be something that's never happened before, so there is no class or manual to tell you how. You will need a deeper understanding of how people and systems work.

Your college education is filled with learnings like this. But you might not always recognize it.

Consider the movie, *The Karate Kid*, in which Mr. Miyagi teaches his student Daniel to train his muscles by painting a fence and waxing cars (and in the remake the student removes and replaces a jacket). Although Daniel does not care about fences or cars, he cares a lot about building the underlying skills that will allow him to meet his own life challenges.

The fences and cars (and jackets) are just a way to practice the underlying skills, which involve building muscle memory that can be used for entirely different tasks in entirely different circumstances.

This idea is not just familiar from the movies. It's the same in sports. The training does not necessarily look like the activity we are training for. Have you ever seen football players training on a tire agility course? There are no tires on the field in a football game, and football players running down the field do not run the same way they run a tire course. But the tire course strengthens knees and ankles, and helps practice changing directions quickly.[19]

So, too, with higher education. When you take courses like *African Architecture* or *The Politics of Museum Displays* – you don't have to care about architecture or museum displays to get a lot out of the class; you just need to practice analyzing the kinds of problems that the course addresses, and proposing or evaluating solutions.

If you hate architecture and love museums, then let yourself be propelled by the emotional energy of that museum passion, by taking the museum course and not the architecture course. But don't

Oh! So the politics of museum displays isn't only about museum displays, but also about general problems, like storytelling, and dealing with critics, and fundraising!

think that either one is only preparing you to be an architect or a museum director; that's not the point at all.

So at the highest level, the answer to the question "What are we supposed to be learning?" is the wisdom of the ages, the gift of prior generations, how the world works, and the meaning of life.

42, right?

At a slightly lower level of abstraction, we are supposed to be learning the five things we already said:

1. How to grow personally and intellectually

2. How to find a role in the workforce

3. The value and means of social mobility

4. The methods of research and innovation

5. The ability to engage productively with others in civic endeavors

More concretely still, there are some specific aptitudes and capabilities that you will need to strengthen. Appendix A describes 26 of these skills: ambiguity tolerance, being open to criticism, building trust, collaboration, conflict management, constructive self-doubt, courage, critical thinking, emotional balance, emotional self-regulation, empathy, focusing your attention, ignoring chaos, independence, initiative, making hard choices, managing competing priorities, persistence, personal discipline, problem solving, project management, relationship building, social awareness, strategic thinking, staying calm under pressure, and willingness to fail.

But that's not a complete list. You also need issue spotting, moral thinking, communication, historical analysis, understanding human motivation, understanding agency versus structure, learning how to learn, defense against propaganda, inspiring others, and many others.[20]

These are the kinds of skills that employers consistently recite when asked what they are looking for, in survey after survey. For example, the World Economic Forum's list of skills employers will be looking for in 2025[21] includes innovation, active learning, problem-solving, critical thinking, resilience, stress tolerance, flexibility, creativity, originality, initiative, self-management, working with people, leadership, social influence, persuasion, systems analysis, and emotional intelligence.

College builds muscle memory for these skills a thousand ways by challenging you with difficult situations. The actual content of your paper on the geography of human migration might be important, but maybe not as important as having to research and write it, clearly and effectively, to a deadline, within certain constraints, based on some ambiguous information, and possibly with conflicting authority, requiring some consultation, incorporating feedback, and then having to present it, while juggling other priorities.

None of the aptitudes we are after is tied to a specific discipline. Take, for example, Communication. Poets and artists communicate differently from science writers and politicians, but they are all drawing from the same principles.

That's why it doesn't much matter what you major in. Even though there is a specific major called "Communications," you will still learn about communicating no matter which discipline you approach it from.

It doesn't matter what I major in?

Similarly, History majors don't have a monopoly on historical analysis – disciplines like literature, art, politics, cultural studies, and science are all deeply interested in history.

You can't learn these dozens of skills very well by studying just one thing. You may love engineering or history, but if all you take are engineering or history classes, you will be missing out on too many different perspectives. Your understanding won't be broad enough to make sense of the challenges coming your way if you do not also at least have some familiarity with language, literature, ethics, economics, and many other disciplines.

That's why breadth requirements or general education requirements mandate that you take a significant number of courses outside your major.

You can measure how serious your college is about educating its students by whether they invest heavily in breadth, or instead allow career-oriented majors to swallow up most of a student's time. The number of classes you take outside your major is also a measure of how serious you are as a student.

At the same time, your college education must also teach you tenacity, detail orientation, and the ability to understand deeply. That's why majors exist, and it's the reason your education would be worse if you only took G.E. classes and did not have a major. Majors allow you to focus hard and truly master one part of the problem. That ability is important, no matter which part of the problem you look at.

Do you see why majors exist, and why they are important? Their primary purpose is not to deliver vocational skills, even if sometimes they can be used that way.

Notice as well that "what we are trying to learn" has very little to do with memorizing boatloads of facts. The world's facts are largely collected in places like Wikipedia. You can have all the facts you want any time, fast and free. Your brain will never beat Wikipedia at storing and retrieving factual information.

But here's the key: Wikipedia doesn't know what all those facts mean -- what are the implications, what should we do, how should we go about it, and how we should weigh the costs and balance the risks?

That's what we are trying to learn at college.

How does a major matter?

What do you mean by "It doesn't matter what you major in?" My parents sure think it does!

And yet the unimportance of your choice of major seems evident, doesn't it? Everyone gets the same degree, a Bachelor's Degree, no matter what they major in. And all the leadership and self-management skills, and self-knowledge, can be learned within any major. When you bet on a career matching your major, you are betting that you won't change careers. But most people don't end up where they planned, and then they rely heavily on the general skills they picked up in GE classes and extra-curricular activities. For those general skills, as well as the self-knowledge and character that a liberal arts education offers, all the majors are the same and it doesn't matter which one you choose.

Aren't majors about choosing a career?

Wait a second, just about everyone chooses a major in an area that they want to be their vocation. Is everyone in the world wrong, or are you wrong?

First, lots of people major in things that they don't intend to be their career. Check how many lawyers majored in "Pre-Law," or how many literature majors become writers or literary critics. Way less than half.[22]

Law schools are stuffed with students who majored in arts, natural sciences, and humanities. Philosophy majors get into medical school all the time, if they also meet the requirements for medical school admission. Indeed, one of your authors majored in Philosophy and was accepted to Medical School.

Studying only sciences in anticipation of medical school is a choice, not a requirement, and it is not a very good choice, either, because physicians do a lot more than just diagnose and treat patients.

But whether we are wrong or right about this is exactly the kind of difficult question that college is going to train your mind to analyze. For the time being, just consider that we might be right, and allow the argument to unfold. We'll get to the bottom of this in Chapter 10.

I'm getting a degree in STEM for a job

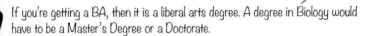

The whole reason I'm going to college is to get a degree in biology so I can get a job in biology. So nothing is more important than my Biology major, right?

If you're getting a BA, then it is a liberal arts degree. A degree in Biology would have to be a Master's Degree or a Doctorate.

It's important to know some biology if you want a job in a lab, but as we will see in Chapter 10, you do not have to major in it. The way your Bachelor's Degree in the Liberal Arts is really going to help you succeed at work is by teaching you everything else you also have to know to succeed – courage, persistence, balancing priorities, empathy, and the other skills we have been talking about, some of which are in Appendix A. If you get a B.S., that's likely going to be narrower and more vocationally focused. You might be missing some of the broader benefits of a B.A.

Classes outside my major

I like aviation, and my goal is to run an airport. Why do I have to take classes like "Folklore," that have nothing to do with my goals?

A Bachelor of Arts degree is not a vocational degree, so it is mostly not about the technical skills you need to do any job. Instead, you are getting the broad, general skills necessary to run anything in general – including an airport – but nothing in particular.

A Master's Degree can get you specific skills focused on specific jobs. Your Bachelor's degree will prepare you for that by giving you a solid foundation of general knowledge and skills that will help you succeed no matter what career or advanced degree you pursue.

Aviation knowledge is important, but you need other things, too. Demand of your Bachelor's degree much more than just technical knowledge.

Building muscle memory

Explain again how writing papers is like building muscle memory?

You are not puzzling over the role of social class in The Great Gatsby just because the answer is worth knowing. You are also practicing thinking about problems like this, and developing muscle memory in the skills necessary to work out a plausible answer to problems like this, including brainstorming, researching, organizing, writing, editing, and interpretation. If you do it enough times, then when books and ideas come at you in the future, you will be much better at understanding what they might have to say.

Gatsby will also introduce you to some characters and problems that you might encounter in real life, and which are likely worth your attention. So the skills you are practicing in the course of building muscle memory for thinking are valuable, and the content of the courses is also separately valuable.

What are "Liberal Arts"?

Why do you keep saying "Liberal Arts?" What does being liberal have to do with this?

Liberal means "free," as in liberating your mind. Liberal Arts are those disciplines that help you develop a **broad perspective** in the world and its diversity, a **flexible mind** that can adapt to uncertainty and develop meaningful interpretations, and a **sense of curiosity** that can inspire discovery, innovation, and lifelong learning.

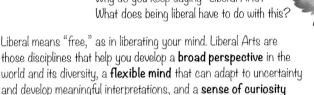

Leadership in college

I did not take any leadership classes in college. I don't even remember any classes called that or about that. But I did do some leadership things – sometimes organizing events, or just doing my share in a club. Clubs most of all teach you that if you don't do it, then it doesn't happen. That's sort of intimidating, but sort of empowering, too. It's a small kind of leadership, but over time I felt myself grow more confident.

Getting to decide

In high school, you needed permission and oversight for everything. In college, you can just decide to do something, like creating a club or an event. It's not so formal, and not so regulated. And there is even money available to help with some kinds of things, if you ask. But you have to ask. That's one of the things I learned in college. Everything takes at least a little bit of money – to buy materials or equipment or whatever. But there's money around. You have to find out how things get funded, and then make a pitch. Sometimes it works.

Chapter 5

Takeaways

- College teaches you dozens of skills in areas like thinking, communicating, self-management, and interpersonal effectiveness

- "Interpersonal effectiveness" is not the name of the class, but doing class assignments nonetheless builds "muscle memory" for how to manage a variety of difficult situations

- No matter what you major in, you will still be building all the same general skills

Chapter 6

Skipping College to Focus on Earnings

We hope to convince readers that there are much more valuable things to be had from college than money, so although increased earning capacity is important, it should not be the sole focus.

But we surely have not convinced everybody, and the ones who believe "college = money or no dice" keep up their sleeve a powerful financial argument.

They argue that even if a good college education leads to greater earning capacity somewhere in the future, that won't make up for the four years that could have been spent earning $100,000 from working, and avoiding $100,000 in college-related expenses. So college graduates start out $200,000 in the hole, and can never catch up financially with those who skipped college entirely.

Hey that's right!

Checkmate!

It is a seductive argument. And whatever the real numbers are (some schools cost even more, and most students are subsidized and don't pay the full sticker price), there is no doubt that those who skip college avoid a significant expense and may have banked years worth of earnings by the time their college-bound friends graduate.

Our answer to this challenge is that you need a college education for all kinds of reasons besides earning capacity – including personal and intellectual growth, and finding your path in life. And don't forget developing your civic skills: society needs you to have a college education for reasons that matter more than anyone's income. The college you're thinking about skipping was built for you, and turning it down to get an entry-level salary for four extra years would be a great tragedy for all involved.

But those who assert this argument may not accept a response based on personal growth or civic value. They want us to show them the money, so show them we shall.

For every story of a Steve Jobs who dropped out of college to start a business and did well, there is another story of an Elizabeth Holmes[23] who dropped out of college to start a business and went to jail because she did not learn some things that college might have taught her.

And there are a hundred more stories about people who dropped out of college to start a business but did not yet know enough about how to run things – how to manage risk, how to navigate complexity, how to make hard decisions – and their businesses went out of business.

When people successfully do things without first learning how to do them, it always makes headlines, and we all read those headlines. But don't be fooled into thinking that those are typical cases.

Just looking at the statistics alone, the most successful leaders in all fields are overwhelmingly more likely to have a college education than is the average population.[24]

And they aren't just getting rich. There are plenty of examples of millionaires who skipped college, made a lot of money, then went on to publish widely read but foolish opinion pieces that a first-year critical thinking class might tear to shreds. They should have taken the class.

The pursuit of money without also developing knowledge and wisdom leads to what Carl Sagan called "a combustible mixture of ignorance and power"[25] that in the end harms everyone.

But if we just have to do the hard math, it comes with a hard truth. The pay disparity between leaders and workers has never been greater.[26] Those four years of entry level salary vanish like a snowflake in the sun compared to a few weeks of CEO pay, or a few months of senior executive pay.

Making the jump from worker to leader is the best financial move you can make.

What the anti-college people are arguing is that they can learn more about leadership by working in a real vocational setting for four years than they can by going to college for four years.

And for some people it will prove to be true.

But statistically speaking, it's a bad bet. And even those who win the bet by skipping college and getting rich anyway usually do not recover all the other things that college offered that no entry level job ever could.

That leaves them, at best, richer in one way, but poorer in many others. Indeed, college graduates overall are happier and healthier, they maker smarter decisions, and they are better off in many different ways, even when controlling for income.[27]

The far likelier outcome for those who skip college to work is that, like the hare in Aesop's fable, the college drop-outs jump to a quick financial lead, but in the end, the tortoises who made the most of their college education beat them every time,[28] in every way.

Don't take our word for it; just look at the statistics. College graduates earn $1 million more in lifetime earnings than those with only a high school diploma.[29] They earn more, no matter what they study. The farther out you look, the greater the difference – even if they started out behind.[30]

And that's an average weighed down by the college students who just partied. The serious students like you, who took the time to read this book, and who knew to approach college as we describe, make even more money, if they so choose.

Making money without going to college

Your "hard numbers" don't prove that I can't make more money by skipping college. In fact, you admitted the opposite, that some people skip college and get rich.

That's right. You might get there either way.

All I showed was that the skills you need to make a lot of money include deep knowledge and a wide variety of leadership skills that college is ready to teach you. And if you acquire those skills, you will be able to apply them to all sorts of endeavors.

You might pick them up on your own. But statistically speaking, it's a bad bet.

And if you actually took statistics, you would understand the reason that it is a bad bet, which has to do with populations. If you only focus on the one prominent person who succeeded on this path, you will miss a thousand who tried but failed.

Maybe you'll be the one.

College doesn't tell you how to balance the odds. But it can help you calculate them realistically.

Disagreeing with parents

I had one agenda for college and my parents had a totally different one. They were the ones paying so they got to decide. Every year I got more interested in my friends' classes, but I never changed majors. I graduated, I got a job. I did okay. But over time, I grew more sorry about what I had missed. My job became a career, then I had kids. There was never a chance to go back. I still read a lot, but it's not a do-over. I don't feel like I eventually got to the same place.

Changing plans

I went to college with a clear plan in mind – I was going to study business in order to make money. The whole thing came unraveled, and that was probably for the best. I was studying accounting, and I just didn't care. I probably would have graduated with C's, if at all. I was stressed and depressed and conflicted. Finally I decided that it would be better to switch my major to Human Development and get good grades in something that wasn't about a career than bad grades in something that was about a career. Funny thing, though: Even though I didn't major in business, I still ended up in business: I manage a tour company.

Chapter 6
Takeaways

- Some people skip college so they can start making money immediately, and avoid the cost of a college education. They end up financially better off in the short term. And by working, they usually pick up some of the self-management skills that college students are working toward, too

- But in the long-term, college graduates on average match and then surpass non-graduates financially, as well as learning a broader range of skills than are likely to be picked up outside of college, plus the non-graduates also miss some other knowledge and experiences that can lead to greater life satisfaction, longer life, and other non-money advantages

Chapter 7

Getting a Better or Worse Education

If you are feeling a little disoriented right now, perhaps a little overwhelmed, but also a little concerned that this wasn't what you expected, that's good. It means we are on the right track.

You do not go to college because you already know everything. Just the opposite. You need to extend and expand your mental, emotional, and social skills in new ways. By definition, you don't yet know what those ways are.

It's also a good sign if you are encountering unfamiliar ideas. That is exactly the kind of problem that you will be practicing in college.

Disorientation also means that you are understanding the implications of what we are telling you. When you transition from high school to college, you should feel a little bit like Dorothy felt landing in Oz – you have entered a very different world in which new and unfamiliar things are now possible. It is exciting, but also unnerving.

Yet despite all we have promised, college will not transform you. It cannot transform you.

Only you can transform yourself.

And it requires a lot of work. College can help. College is a great place to discover new passions, new truths, new ways of thinking, and new capabilities, that can lead to greater personal fulfillment. You could find your calling. You could achieve an entirely new station in society. You might do something creative and innovative. You could contribute significantly to your community. Everything you need is here.

But you don't have to.

You can pass all your classes and graduate and be essentially unchanged, if you want.

People do that all the time. And then they complain that they didn't learn anything at college, and that society doesn't value a college degree. And they are completely right. They learned very little, and society does not value their degree. And they probably paid a lot of money and got very little for it. It's a tragic story.

But don't blame the college; that was the students' own choice.

College is one of those things where you only get out of it what you put into it.[31] Lots of things in life are like that. What makes college different is that if you throw yourself into it, you can really get a huge amount out of it – an extraordinary return, if you make the investment.

If you don't make the investment, though, you get no return. Making more money after college isn't automatic. The same study that says 80% of college graduates make more, also says that 20% of college graduates do not make more.[32] The "some" that do not make more are not randomly distributed.

There are two types of student who leave college without improved earnings. First, the ones who party or cheat their way through college, or otherwise do not make the investment in learning, and reap no reward.

Second, there are those who leave college but do not enter the paid workforce at all, or choose a path in public interest or the volunteer sector.

They value being educated, but do not use that education to pursue wealth.

So the studies on college earnings are actually weighed down by these college graduates who either did not make the investment in learning and did not gain new skills, or they gained new skills but chose not to use them economically.[33]

That means you can choose to be among the 80% that invest in learning, and do even better than average.

But it's not an easy investment to make. You must devote your two most valuable possessions: your time and your attention.

That is easier said than done.

Imagine that you are traveling through a wood, and you come upon a meadow. In the meadow flows a fountain. It is the fountain of knowledge – all knowledge of all types, every science, every art, every philosophy – the accumulated wisdom of a thousand generations.

Imagine that you are allowed, for a brief time, to drink from the fountain. Would you do it?

Happily!

Now imagine that the fountain of knowledge stands not alone, but is just one of several fountains flowing in the meadow.

You also behold the fountain of drinking and partying, the fountain of interactive video games, the fountain of streaming entertainment, the fountain of social media disputation, the fountain of sexual exploration, the fountain of fraternity and sorority life, and the fountain of trivia. You can drink as much as you want from whichever you want, but only for a short time. Which do you choose?

Now imagine that the fountain of knowledge has the appearance of water: odorless, colorless, tasteless. Essential for life, and containing great secrets of the universe, but the other fountains are colorful and flavorful and beautiful and fun. Is there any chance you would spend much time at the fountain of knowledge?

No way.

Although that story was fiction, the choice you face in allocating your time and attention is real, and don't imagine that it will be easy. Watch how your friends choose, and understand why. Learn from their experience. You are buffeted by all the same forces that they are.

In this respect, your college experience is very much like a fairy tale. You can have all the world's knowledge, with which you might build yourself an extraordinary future in whatever shape you desire, or you can trade it away for some temporary distraction.

Maybe just a little distraction?

Can you have just a little distraction? Sure. As much as you like. That's the challenge.

In the end, you have to decide why you came to college and what you want to get out of it, and how much you care about what version of yourself you find standing beneath the graduation cap a few years hence, or whether you graduate at all.

The good news is that the choice is yours. The bad news is also that the choice is yours.

We hope you choose to get as much out of your college experience as you possibly can, both inside and outside the classroom. We created this book to help you. And we'll show you how.

We are going to cover everything you need to succeed: choosing a college; transitioning to college life; and how to read, write, and think like a college student. We'll look at the expectations for college students, which will be different from high school. We'll review the most common traps students fall into, techniques you can use to stay on track, and we'll talk about how to get help when you need it: academic, emotional, financial, and more.

To summarize and review, if you take college seriously and do it right, you will develop a wide range of important aptitudes and capabilities that will significantly increase your earning capacity because you will be better at running things.

In addition to the money…

You will also be able to discover the paths to personal growth, greater life fulfillment, social mobility, creativity, and civic engagement. You may discover your calling. And you will be able to use the college for the reason it was built: to help you play your part in handing the next generation a civilization in as good a shape or better than when you found it.

For our part, we offer you everything in this book, which will get you off to a good start in college.

But no book can be a replacement for the entire college experience. Just as you can't get healthy by reading about working out, you can't get college smart by reading a summary of what you will learn. You have to learn by doing, practicing with real people, solving real challenges, together.

So now you know why you are going to college, and what you are going to learn. Next we are going to look at some practical considerations, like choosing a college, choosing a major, choosing classes, and how you can chart a good course for yourself.

Choosing a college

But I already chose my college. Are you going to tell me I chose wrong?

No, you can relax. Here's a spoiler for the next chapter: Although some colleges are better than others, and different ones can work for your in different ways, you can get a great education at any college, or a completely inadequate education at any college. It's always up to you.

Chapter 7

Takeaways

- Although your college experience can be transformative in many ways, you have to do the work to make that happen

- Part of that work involves taking the opportunity seriously, and devoting yourself to learning all there is to learn, and not falling victim to the various distractions that are also available, and will use up your time without giving you much of lasting value in return

- Focus on your goals; beware of distractions

Part 3

Preparing for Success

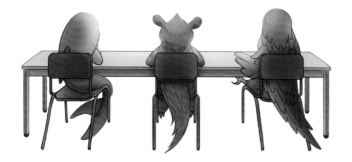

Chapter 8

Choosing Your College

Next we'll look at how to choose a college, in case you haven't already chosen one. If you already know your college, feel free to jump to the next chapter -- unless you're curious about how your college might measure up, in which case, read on!

The three questions you start with are (1) Whether to go, (2) Where to go, and (3) How to pay for it. The problem is immediately complicated, because how to pay for it depends on where you go, and whether to go depends (in part) on how you pay for it.

Quite the conundrum.

Everyone's situation is different, but we can provide ten points of clarity.

1. Elite Schools. The elite, expensive liberal arts colleges are elite and expensive for a reason, and not only because they provide access to a future professional network among the elite. They are also investing a lot of resources in the educational experience in ways that most state schools and community colleges simply cannot. They spend more per student, and that expenditure is heavily subsidized by endowments, so even though they cost more, they are typically a better value.

That doesn't mean that it's worth the extra expense (indeed, most students do not pay the sticker price), or that you can't get a great education elsewhere, but those elite school students have an advantage. At a lesser school, if you work hard, you can do nearly as well and pay a lot less. And, of course, you can also attend the elite school, ignore the opportunities, and enjoy the worst of both worlds: paying a lot more to get a lot less. Keep in mind, too, that if you are aiming at a difficult target, like medical school or an Ivy League graduate school, you'll be facing a headwind if your Bachelor's degree is from an undistinguished school.

2. Student Loan Debt. You do not want to go deeply into debt in order to get a college education. That's not because the college education isn't worth what it costs; it absolutely might be. But you don't want to go deeply into debt for anything. It curtails your future options in ways that defeat the purpose of getting the education in the first place. So think long and hard about splurging on an expensive school, even if it's a really great school. Keep in mind, too, that not every expensive school is good; some are just expensive. Indeed, one study found that the majority of private colleges offered a poor value, at least compared with the elite schools that spend a lot per student but cover a higher percentage of that expense with their endowments rather than tuition.[34]

3. Small Schools. There are good reasons to favor small schools over large schools, especially for undergraduate education, and the biggest one is class size. The best learning rarely occurs in large lecture halls, but more often in smaller discussions and in classes small enough that the instructor can give you meaningful feedback. Average class size matters, as does undergraduate access to seminars (classes with fewer than 20 students, which is typical for graduate classes, but can be hard to find for undergraduates in large universities).

4. Large Schools. There are also good reasons to favor large schools over small schools -- especially for graduate school, but even for undergraduate education. Large schools have more resources to build better facilities, and they attract world class faculty. And often they attract more serious students and more diverse students. You should be very attentive to the kinds of students attracted to the institution. If you want to challenge yourself to do well, surround yourself with other students who have high aspirations and a range of backgrounds. You will learn from each other, not just from the faculty, which supercharges your education.

5. Leadership Opportunities. Which is not to say that there are not advantages to being a big fish in a small pond. If you find yourself at a small school, you have better odds of getting a leadership position in student government and the student newspaper, as well as activities and clubs. You should make the most of those opportunities to practice leadership. But even among the smaller schools, those with a culture of learning are going to help you succeed better than schools with a culture of partying or sports, or a culture of students-who-think-they-are-commuting-in-for-13th-grade.

6. Transfer Students. There can be benefits to starting at a community college and then transferring to a 4-year institution. For example, the first two years might cost less and there might be smaller class sizes. You might choose to study abroad from the community college, leaving more on-campus time at the 4-year college. And a transfer arrangement may be the only economically viable option for some students. However, the research reveals some risk. The transferring students need to have learned at the community college how to be a college student in a way that works at a potentially very different 4-year institution, and by transferring they will lose two years of peer and academic networking that the other students will have.[35] If this is your path, decide where you want to transfer to early, and ask your advisor about any transfer agreements that will ease the transition. You will want to get familiar with and involved in the receiving institution as early as possible. And while you are at the two-year institution be thinking and acting every day like a liberal arts student, even if you find yourself surrounded by vocational students in vocational programs. Choose classes and advisors as if you were already at the 4-year institution.

What is a transfer agreement?

7. High-Ranked Schools. Also, do not be taken in by the high rankings of world famous research universities. Those schools care about research first, and undergraduate learning quite a bit further down the list. Their world famous faculty may not even teach many classes. And even if the famous faculty did teach, they may not be good instructors, because they weren't chosen for that, are not very much evaluated on that, and may not even have been trained for that. For sure, some of those famous faculty members are gifted and inspiring teachers. But some of the best instructors we have ever seen were adjunct lecturers, and some of the worst instructors we have ever seen were tenure track faculty.

Wait, the best schools don't have the best instructors?

8. Campus Atmosphere. Be sure to weigh in the balance how the campus simply feels. You're likely to spend four years there, so you might as well like it – the weather, the mood, residential opportunities, and the places to study. Is it the kind of place that will allow you to think elevated thoughts, or the kind of place that will bore you or stress you out? Is it too close to home, or too far from home, for you to concentrate on your studies? Good campuses will remind you every minute, everywhere you look, that what you are doing there is important.

Elevated thoughts?

9. Special Programs. If you have a peculiar interest, make sure it is compatible with the college you choose. For example, if you are peculiarly interested in astrobiology or digital design, not every school has those programs. Nearly every school does have a Philosophy program, but some Philosophy programs are more robust than others, and the more serious programs are likely to offer a broader range of classes. If you want to go to graduate school at MIT, the path to get there is difficult if you are starting from an undistinguished lower-tier school. It's not impossible, but you want to be realistic about the future impact of your present choices.

10. Academic Policies. The last thing is among the most important to consider, but also among the most difficult to detect, which is whether the college has flexible policies. Can you try out classes, and then add or drop easily, or do they have strict time limits and late fees? Are the classes you care about offered frequently, or only only once every other year? Can you get into the major you want, or is it impacted? Are the breadth requirements strong and flexible, or rigid and limiting? Does the college allow majors that use up most of your units, or does it insist that students have the flexibility to take lots of electives? Is the quality of the academic advising good, or did the college spend less on that? What advantages does this college's study abroad program offer compared to other colleges? These things matter much more than the average SAT score of the incoming class or the acceptance rate, but you'll have difficulty finding out about them.

Those sound like good questions to ask on a campus tour!

There's not much beside that. You might not be able to afford your first choice school, and you might not be accepted to your second

Doesn't average SAT score measure the quality of my fellow students?

choice school. But that's okay. First find a place that works for you financially and emotionally, and then you will be able to make it work academically. You may be prevented from getting the college you want, but no one can prevent you from getting the education you want.

Famous faculty

I thought the whole point of going to a prestigious college was that you would get the smartest faculty, the ones who wrote the text book, so you would learn more from them.

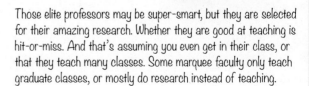

Those elite professors may be super-smart, but they are selected for their amazing research. Whether they are good at teaching is hit-or-miss. And that's assuming you even get in their class, or that they teach many classes. Some marquee faculty only teach graduate classes, or mostly do research instead of teaching.

Good places to study

You said to look for a college that has good places to study. What are good places to study?

Partly it depends on what you like – comfy chairs in a library, secluded study nooks with electricity, or maybe a coffee shop.

And partly it depends on what your study challenge is: You might just need to read, or maybe you're developing a presentation with others, which will want a different environment. Whether you are reading, working with flash cards, editing, writing, reading aloud, doing practice exercises, working on a project or podcast, or listening to or watching course materials -- match the best place to study with the assignment type. Experiment to see what works best. If the residence halls are too chaotic, steer clear.

You might be drawn to a bench under a shade tree – but remember when you tour the campus in summer that your classes will mostly be in colder months, when some climates demand indoor studying.

Community College Transfer Programs

I want to transfer from my community college to the state university, but what is a "transfer program" that I would ask my advisor about?

Also sometimes called a "pipeline" program. It means that the community college knows that many students will want to transfer to a specific college, so they have an agreement with the receiving college to help you make the transition. You might have guaranteed admission and assurance that the credits you have earned will be accepted by the receiving institution. They might also help you plan so you know which courses to take at which institution. And the whole transfer process might be streamlined.

Relying on college rankings

What's wrong with relying on the SAT scores of incoming students? Didn't you say we should surround ourselves with students who would challenge our thinking?

Yes, but there are often better factors to consider than the easy-to-measure statistics used in college rankings.

Suppose you want to take a vacation at a National Park, and you are trying to decide between Zion in Utah, Everglades in Florida, or Volcanoes in Hawaii.

You want to consider what's available at each destination, and especially whether you want to be in a desert, in a swamp, or on an island.

The thing you probably will care less about is the average annual income of the other visitors to the park. You'll do better focusing on things that are directly related to the experience you are going to have.

With colleges, that might be things like graduation rate, amount spent per student, number of full-time faculty allocated to the disciplines you care about, whether it is easy to explore different courses without having to commit too early, whether access to popular majors is restricted, and whether there are good housing and transportation options for those who cannot live on campus.[36] On your campus visit, ask about those kinds of things, even if the college would rather talk about its mascot and the Nobel prize winners you will never study with.

Great facilities

I had no idea how to choose a college. I ended up focusing on one that had great facilities, and even a bowling alley; I thought that was cool. In the whole four years I never went bowling once.

Staying close to home

I chose to go to college close to home, and that worked out for me. I am very close to my family, so it was good to be within driving distance. But I was still far enough away that I felt like I was independent and had left home. I have to admit that part of my goal was to keep my high school friends, and a boyfriend, but that didn't really happen. My boyfriend and I broke up anyway, and I ended up feeling closer to my new friends than my old friends.

Confronting insecurity

I was actually frightened by all the things I had to do at college, because there were so many. But by the end of first year, I was like, You got this! And I started to relax. There were lots of important things to do, but not a single one was beyond my capabilities. It was just a matter of facing up to it. And everyone was there to help me. College started by challenging my confidence, but ended up improving it.

Discovering the library

I discovered the library for studying, and wow, has it made a difference. I used to think I had attention deficit disorder, but now I am not sure – I may have been the one distracting myself. All I need are my books, and notebook, and a pen. Our library is very quiet, so it's easy to focus, I can get so much done so quickly compared to how I used to study. I thought I wouldn't like just sitting with myself, but I love it – or at least I love getting my work done. I didn't believe that studying in a quiet place would be helpful, or even tolerable, until I tried it.

Chapter 8
Takeaways

- You should choose your college carefully, because there are lots of different factors to consider, and the most important factors are poorly expressed by the popular college rankings

- You should not go deeply in debt to go to college, even if it's a really great college

- You can get a great education at any college if you put in the work, or you can get a poor education even at a great college, if you don't put in the work

Chapter 9

Before You Get To College

Right from the start, have reasonable expectations about what it takes to get the most out of the college experience.

Required Equipment

Doing any job requires that you have the right tools and that you actually use them. If you're in construction, you would look comical trying to build a house with a pocket knife, wielding it variously as a hammer, saw, and screwdriver.

Higher education requires tools for managing and processing information – computers, books, and software for research, composition, and collaboration.

Computers. Do not try to go to college on your phone; you need at least a laptop. The amount and type of information you are going to be considering and creating does not fit on a phone.

A tablet computer, like an iPad®, could be very helpful. Tablets are optimized for reading, and you are going to be doing a lot of reading. But a tablet will not be a great replacement for a laptop. You are trying to think big thoughts, and complex thoughts. It takes space. Ideally, plug your laptop into an external screen. Maybe two. Opening your mind and expanding your horizon are harder to do in a cramped visual space.

Your college knows you need this equipment, and they may be able to help. The library is a great place to start looking for these. Check for

I can read fine on my phone!

programs that allow you to borrow or rent (including long-term rentals) not only computers and tablets, but all sorts of audio visual equipment. Find out how to check out anything you need but don't have.

Productivity Applications. You need a writing program (like Microsoft Word or Google Docs or Apple's Pages), and a calendar, and a to-do list. There are free ones available, and fancier ones. It's okay to do some of this in print, but your to-do list in particular needs to be with you at all times. We'll talk later about how to use these productivity tools.

Books. Read the assigned texts. We'll talk later about how to read effectively, but right now let's be clear that you have to at least have the books. Textbooks can be very expensive; unreasonably expensive. Don't get us started on the academic publishing industry. Nonetheless, if you don't have the books, and you don't read the books, then you are not actively interacting with the thoughts in those books. If the assigned books are too expensive, check the library or buy used books online (and be ready for longer shipping times). Ebooks sometimes cost less, and the built-in search feature may match your study style.

Good place to study. You may be under the impression that you can think clearly in a noisy, crowded, cluttered environment with music playing. But most people cannot. Finding the best environment for studying takes practice. Try out different kinds of places. The libraries are filled with places optimized for contemplation. Learn how to use libraries this way. You likely can also reserve study rooms, even group study rooms. Find out how, and find a number of such places on campus, and use them.

That's not a lot of equipment, but it's really important. You should not make any exceptions to the list above.

Habits

There are a lot of good habits that will help you through college, too. If you haven't developed them, start right now. It's never too soon or too late to develop a good habit, and the benefits can last a lifetime. Begin here:

Review the Programs. You should be familiar with the majors available, and courses within each area of study. Explore the course schedule when it is released each semester – not just the areas of study that you know you are interested in, also the ones that you do not yet know that you are interested in, or that your friends are interested in.

Study the Course Syllabus. The course syllabus is your roadmap or GPS. The syllabus includes everything that you are supposed to learn during the course. You might be surprised how much more effectively your mind can synthesize what's coming at it if you know in advance what's coming and why. The syllabus also includes important details about the culture of this particular class – everyone's expectations for everyone else. And certainly be aware of the course policies, including for attendance and extensions.

Master the Courseware. Most colleges use some learning management system similar to Moodle® or Canvas®, where course materials are posted and discussions are managed. You need to know how each professor is expecting you to interact – are they posting videos that you are supposed to be watching, quizzes that you are supposed to be completing, discussions that you are supposed to be joining, or articles that you are supposed to be downloading? Maybe you need to work through a multi-step module that requires you to complete a number of tasks. And check the courseware often. The course syllabus will be here, and it may get adjusted during the course, just like your GPS headings update when road conditions change. Different professors may approach this differently, which can be frustrating, but it allows you to practice with different learning approaches and with being adaptable.

Attend Class. It is your job to make the most of your education. Skipping class is a bad idea. If you don't want to attend your classes, then you might not be ready for college.

If the class is boring, then you may have chosen the wrong class, the wrong professor, or even the wrong major, and you can learn from that. But mostly you should not be shifting to the college or the professor the job of engaging or entertaining you. You are responsible for learning, and that means being responsible for finding the important skills and knowledge that are being offered in your class.

Attending class is also a form of networking. You are connecting with your professor and your peers, and those relationships may be helpful right now for clarifying and understanding the class requirements and homework assignments, or if you need help studying or reviewing the course materials. And these relationships can help later on, too, when advancing your career.

The very worst case scenario is that you are trapped in a room where unimportant material is being presented in an uninteresting way. That

But what if I have a conflict?

Practice being bored? You gotta be kidding me.

should be very unusual, but it could happen. It certainly happens outside of college. Practice handling that situation, which means making the best of it, not fleeing and blaming others. Not everything that is important is also entertaining, or even interesting. Learn it anyway.

Some students believe that if they sit in the classes and do what they are told, then they will become educated. And then they are resentful when they get weak grades, even though they worked hard and did what they were told. But a college grade isn't for obedience. It is for successfully engaging with the material. In a very real sense, you are educating yourself. Just listening to the professor speak and memorizing what they say won't get you even half-way there.

Take Good Notes. The human mind can only hold things in short-term or working memory for at most a few minutes. So if you attend class for an hour or so, the moment the class ends you will already have forgotten most of what happened. Taking notes serves two purposes. First, it focuses your mind and helps you remember more. Second, it creates a record of things that you will otherwise forget. Reviewing that record can help you remember. If the professor gives you slides or notes in advance, those will be a great record of things that you would have forgotten, but still take your own notes to focus your mind and help you remember more. Saundra McGuire's *Teach Yourself How to Learn*[37] explains how to take good notes, study better, and learn more.

Check your Email. You may prefer texting or other communication channels, but universities (and your future employers) are likely to rely heavily on email, and they will

Isn't it the college's job to communicate with me, and shouldn't the college choose the methods that I prefer?

expect you to do so, too. Important notices will come via email, and sometimes urgent information. You must stay on top of that. Not knowing information sent by email is not an excuse for missed deadlines. Treat email as part of your job and learn how to keep an organized folder system for emails.

Finish assignments early. Saving work until the last minute is a bad habit, and finishing college work a week in advance is a good habit. You don't directly get extra points for finishing early, but if you finish early you will have additional chances to review your work before you turn it in. We have never written anything that could not have been improved by an additional read. And it's especially easy to spot errors and ambiguities a day or so later, when the written thoughts are not so fresh in your mind. So finish early, giving yourself multiple opportunities for additional drafts. The more chances you give yourself to make the writing better, the better the writing will get.

But that's not even the best reason to finish assignments early. Things come up. Things take longer than you expect. Half-way through you realize you have an unanswered question, or that you don't understand one of the readings. Maybe your best friend is having a crisis. Give yourself extra time to handle unexpected trouble by starting early and finishing early.

Get Enough Sleep. The science is very clear[38] that poor sleep impairs your mental abilities, even if you think you are fine and you feel fine. The whole point of college is to improve your thinking. If you are sleep deprived, it will take a lot of effort just to get your cognitive processes up to normal. Give yourself a tail wind, not a head wind.

Check the Ratings on Your Professors. Many colleges give awards to superior instructors. Find

No way. I work best under pressure. Plus, I like the adrenaline rush of getting something in just before the deadline.

This is good life advice, too!

But there aren't enough hours in the day! Time spent sleeping takes away from things I care about more.

out who has been nominated. The quality of the instructor matters immensely and varies greatly. It will even make sense to find the best instructors and see what they are teaching that might interest you.

Also, a course that interests you may be taught by different faculty members at different times, and you get to choose which professor you get. Check the student evaluations wherever you can find them (colleges do not tend to make these available to students, but some publicly available websites offer faculty ratings). Don't just look at the ratings: some students give five stars for an easy A, and one star to professors who hold them accountable to learn something. That's the opposite of what you are looking for. Instead, you want to see whether the course is reasonably demanding, well-organized, and intellectually engaging. Often you can detect this from the reviewers' comments.

Build Relationships with Faculty. Every professor is a potential mentor. Plus, you will need recommendations for jobs and internships, for campus awards and scholarships, or if you are going on to graduate or professional school. The faculty are looking for serious students that put in the effort and that care about learning. You can demonstrate that by talking to faculty members and learning from your conversations. Most faculty like talking to students – you are the main reason that they are there!

Myth Busting

Some misinformation about the college experience is particularly widespread. False things seem true if you hear them often enough, so these myths are especially important to debunk. Here are some hard truths:

Limit the Partying. Part of what you are learning at college involves social interactions. You won't get a complete education if you go to the library and climb inside your books for four years. Humans are social, and life is social, and there is much to learn from the people around you. But it's also easy to overdo it. The myth is that all kids party. Only about half of college students participate in underage drinking.[39] In Chapter 13, we'll talk about balancing competing priorities. For now, just keep in mind that time spent partying is time not spent on other things you also care about.

But what if partying IS what I care about? What if I want to have a career as a party planner?

Multi-tasking does not work. Focus your attention. Most people think they are pretty good at multi-tasking, but scientists have looked at this hard, and the evidence shows, overwhelmingly, that no human is good at multi-tasking.[40] Even if you are better at multi-tasking than others, you are still worse off than when you do not multi-task. Multitasking lowers productivity, slows task completion, and decreases task quality. Multi-tasking feels efficient. It feels like you are getting two things done for the price of one. The reality is the opposite. You are getting less than two half-things for the price of one, because your speed, depth of comprehension, and attention to detail are badly impaired. And in college, those matter a lot.

I disagree. I can't concentrate without the TV on, or at least music playing.

Pulling all-nighters is not a flex, it's a failure. So for the same reason that finishing assignments well before they are due is a good habit, pulling all-nighters is a bad habit. If you find yourself pulling an all-nighter, it probably means that you are not managing your time well enough. If your friends are frequently pulling all-nighters, or are proud of it, then worry about whether they are exposing you to other bad

No one WANTS to pull an all-nighter, but sometimes it's necessary, no?

habits. Unanticipated situations can arise that call for heroic action; it should be rare.

Artificial Intelligence Services like ChatGPT Are Dangerous. You are at college

to strengthen your thinking abilities, and that means you have to do the work yourself. You wouldn't send a robot to the gym to do your full body workout; that would defeat the entire purpose of exercising. Similarly, if you want to strengthen your mind, you can't delegate the thinking to a computer.

If the AI writes an A+ paper for you, you risk getting thrown out of college for cheating. But even if you could get away with cheating your fellow students and the institution, you won't get away from having cheated yourself. When a future employer is looking for the college-level skills that you were supposed to have developed while earning your Bachelor's degree, and they don't find them, your career will stall by that much, and your fake GPA won't help you.

You're forgetting that I can use AI at my job, too, so there's no problem preparing for that job by using AI in college first!

Chapter 22 covers how you should and should not use AI in college.

Double Majoring Does Not Make Sense

Ambitious students often imagine that if their major demonstrates expertise, then a double-major represents greater achievement. It doesn't work like that.

A hat may protect you from the sun, but stacking two hats provides no greater benefit and actually can cause troubles. So it is with stacking majors. The second major constrains your course selection, but does not improve the value of your credential. In fact, it makes your degree less valuable, because you have unnecessarily spent time satisfying major requirements that reduce the breadth of your education and prevent you from exploring disciplines that might have really been helpful.

If what you're hoping for is a boost to your resume, consider adding a "relevant coursework" section that can highlight specific courses in alignment with a job, which can become talking points in an interview.

Work or play?

Whoa! You make college sound like hard work, and not much fun!

It's not just hard work, it's important work, and should not be taken lightly.

Too much fun?

So we shouldn't have fun?

Yes, you should have fun. Indeed, college should introduce you to new and better ways to experience fun. Some parts of your education will be enormously enjoyable, Relish that, and allow yourself some fun as a way of energizing you for harder challenges. But if having fun is a higher priority than learning, then you won't get as much out of college as you could.

Attending boring classes

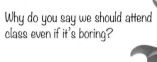

Why do you say we should attend class even if it's boring?

First, even if you aren't learning as much as you want, you will still learn more by attending than by not attending. Second, you're responsible for learning; the college only promises to be educational, not entertaining. Third, in real life, many important things that you need to learn will be important but not entertaining. If you can't learn difficult material, you will miss many important things. This is your chance to learn how to learn even when it is more difficult.

Attendance not required

If attendance isn't required for my grade, that means the school agrees I don't need to attend.

No, it doesn't mean that. The grade isn't your learning. If you just focus on grades, you'll make just that kind of mistake, trading away your learning for something worth less.

You attend because that's how you learn, and the learning is why you are there. Good grades will follow naturally, but chase the learning, don't chase the grade.

Attending online classes

How do I "attend" a class that is online and asynchronous?

You need to get to know the online learning platform really well. Click through every page that is available. Read everything. Find the syllabus, find the grades, find the readings. Bookmark the most important pages so you can get back to them easily.

Also, you need to create touch points with your professor. If your professor offers office hours, go to them. Treat that as part of the class. And if they don't have office hours, develop questions about the class every week or so and set up time to talk to your professor about those question. Do this so you can get to know them and they can get to know you, even though the class doesn't meet in person.

You will find that every professor uses the online learning system differently. It will look different for every class. This is a lesson in adapting to different teaching styles. Later, in the workplace, you will have to adapt to different management styles from various supervisors. Practice that now.

Just here for the degree

Hard pass on all this garbage. I just want the degree, because I can't go up a level in my job without it. I'm not doing any extra.

Don't be so sure that the degree is all you need, and not the underlying education. I understand that they said you just need the degree. But does that really make sense?

Use your college education to ask why they care if you spent four years in college? Why do they think that is so important that they would put a hard ceiling on your career if you have not done it?

Maybe you're right. Maybe they are just trying to weed out people who lack the time and money to go to college. But isn't it more likely that they think you will inevitably learn important skills that are necessary to perform at the next level?

And if you manage to be one of the few who get the degree without the learning, are you sure they won't know? Meeting the minimum requirement only gives you a chance to succeed in the job. It doesn't guaranty your success. You might need that education after all.

Partying for a career

Does big-time partying work for future professional party planners?

One of the things you are learning in college is not to fool yourself. Party planners are successful if they are good planners; it is their customers who do the partying.

Listening to music while studying

You don't really mean that I study worse when music is playing, do you? My experience is just the opposite.

The research shows that music increases productivity for non-cognitive, boring, repetitive tasks, like laying bricks. For complex or cognitively challenging tasks, music takes a serious toll.[41] Reading comprehension is impaired even by music you like, even by music with no lyrics.[42] The subjective experience you are describing has to do with your comfort, not your effectiveness.

All Nighters

Admit it: Sometimes it really is necessary to pull an all-nighter.

That depends on what you mean by "necessary." If you delay long enough or misjudge the amount of time required, then it becomes necessary, but you are the one who made it that way. The instances when unforeseeable problems emerge that could not have been planned for or guarded against are indeed rare.

Who gets the blame?

It feels like you're saying that I am responsible for everything that happens to me. But bad things happen that I can't control. Why should I be blamed for my situation? It makes me anxious just thinking about it.

You are right, we mostly do not control the situations in which we find ourselves, and many misfortunes are not our fault. The world is full of difficulties and bad luck.

But how we respond to the situations in which we find ourselves – that really is up to us. So if you got yourself into a difficult situation, you will first want to learn how to avoid letting that happen again. But the part that you still control is this: What are you going to do about it? That's on you.

College can't eliminate life's uncertainties, but college can give you the knowledge and ability to respond to difficult situations more effectively than by merely experiencing anxiety.

Reading without reading

It turns out that I went to college with really poor learning habits. I didn't need them at high school – I got okay grades without good study habits – so I didn't develop them. I didn't even know that I wasn't doing it right, until first year at college, when I found myself floundering, and didn't know why. In the end, all I had to do was to change my expectations about how hard everything was. I had to stop being so sure I understood what I was reading. Just because I read it, didn't mean I understood it yet – I had to learn to watch for that gap.

My double-major

I thought double-majoring was like Beast Mode for college. While my friends were taking interesting electives like literature and language, I was knuckling down under double-major requirements that barely gave me enough room to do the minimum GEs. I liked that, because it felt like I was focusing harder and they were being trivolous. It wasn't until I was a junior that I realized what I was missing. My career ended up being in administration of operations. It had nothing to do with either of my majors.

Deciding whether to party

I didn't go to college to party, but my new friends were doing it, and it was fun, and sometimes daring. My first quarter grades were lower than I am used to, which ended up being a wakeup call for me. I had to decide what I cared about, and put my time and attention there. That got me back on track.

Chapter 9
Takeaways

- You need good equipment and good habits to do well in college

- Don't try to get by on your phone; you need a computer

- Read the books, do the assignments, attend class, get enough sleep, and find a good place to study

- Finish assignments early

- Multi-tasking doesn't work, and that includes listening to music while studying. You must practice focusing your attention

- Don't let an AI do your learning for you

- Double-majors can seriously reduce the breadth of your education

Chapter 10

Majors and Careers

We said earlier that you should major in whatever interests you, because the relationship between majors and careers is not what most students think. The data is clear. Review the charts in Appendix B to see for yourself. Here is what you will find:

The Census Bureau keeps educational statistics on employment, including what people majored in, and what they ended up doing.[43] You'll be surprised by what you see in the most recent data (2020 census).

For example, most STEM majors don't end up working in STEM. In fact, less than one-third. Even for those who major in engineering, two-thirds do not work as engineers.

Perhaps even more surprising, although most people in STEM careers majored in STEM, you don't have to major in STEM to have a career in STEM. About one-fourth of people working in STEM did not major in STEM. That doesn't mean they didn't study STEM at all, or they don't know anything about it. But you don't have to major in it, and many do not.

The opposite of that is that those who major in Literature, Liberal Arts, History, Arts, or Communication demonstrate extraordinary flexibility, and are about evenly divided among a large array of careers, including sales, service, construction, production, arts, education, legal, social services, business, and management.

In fact, people enter management from all majors. Only about half of business majors end up in either business or management[44], and fewer than half of the people who ended up in management majored in business. Instead, managers are drawn from all majors, including computers, engineering, physical sciences, social sciences, psychology, education, literature, liberal arts, communications, and more.

It's true that more business majors go into business than other majors, but that's because their interest lies there. The major is not a requirement. People from all majors go into business. Their non-business major does not prevent them from doing so.

And there are more surprises, too. For example, students who major in computer science expecting an easy time getting a job actually have a slightly higher unemployment rate than those with majors like Philosophy and Linguistics. That's because every kind of vocational training program, coding academy, and software boot camp offers to teach people programming skills. Plus, software developers from around the world working as contractors for global software development firms add to the fierce competition for coding jobs.

By contrast, mastering a foreign language, as you might in many Area Studies majors, automatically qualifies you for a variety of jobs. If it is a commonly spoken language, then there may be many jobs. If it is an unusual language, then you may be uniquely qualified.

That doesn't mean that you shouldn't major in engineering if you want to be an engineer. But check the job postings for careers you care about and see if they require a particular major. Usually not.

Most important, understand that the job market changes, and people frequently – more often than not – end up somewhere different from where they expected. One study measured an average of 12.6 different jobs over people's work-life.[45] It's not something you can easily plan for.

As a result, for most students, it will be wise to build flexible skills for an uncertain future, rather than bet big that you and the job market will agree on things a few years down the road.

Are you surprised by the power and value of a flexible major? You may have been told that STEM careers have higher starting salaries. But keep in mind that starting salary isn't lifetime salary, and the credentials you need for career entry are not the same as the skills you need for career advancement. Therefore, many of the studies you see that correlate major with starting salary are measuring the wrong thing. The studies that look at earnings 15 years out tell a different story.

Moreover, these studies mostly do not look at which courses people actually took, how well they did in those courses, ability, interest, motivation, or socioeconomic status. Once those are accounted for, more than half the economic difference among majors vanishes. Choice of major has some impact on economic outcome, but the impact is not extreme.[46]

All this is not to say that what you learn in your major is irrelevant to your career prospects. Many careers require technical training, and some of that technical training can be had at four-year colleges.

What we are saying instead is that (1) you can usually get the technical training you need without committing to a complete major, and (2) many of the skills you will need to succeed in any career will have to be learned outside the major.

Therefore, students are over-emphasizing college major as a component of career success, and under-emphasizing other types of learning.

If we are right about this, then we are likely to find senior executives who majored in the liberal arts, and we do so find. For example,

- Hewlett Packard CEO Carly Fiorina majored in **Medieval History and Philosophy**

- Lyft CEO David Risher majored in **Comparative Literature**

- Home Depot CEO Ted Decker majored in **English**

- Southwest Airlines CEO Herb Kelleher **majored in English**

- American Express CEO Ken Chenault majored in **History**

- Avon CEO Andrea Jung majored in **English Literature**

- Campbell's CEO Denise Morrison majored in **Psychology**

- PopSockets CEO David Barnett majored in **Philosophy**

- ACLU President Deborah Archer majored in **Government**

- The Walt Disney Company CFO Christine McCarthy majored in **Biology**

- GE Vice Chair and Hulu co-founder Beth Comstock majored in **Biology**

- Netflix founder Reed Hastings majored in **Mathematics**

- Flickr & Slack founder Stewart Butterfield majored in **Philosophy**

- Host Hotels CEO Ed Walter majored in **Political Science**

- Kellogg CEO Steve Cahillane majored in **Political Science**

- Delta Airlines CEO Richard Anderson majored in **Political Science**

- Albuquerque Mayor Tim Keller majored in **Art History**

- Chipotle CEO Steve Ells majored in **Art History**

You can find as many of these as you want.

The point is not that if you want to be Mayor of a city like Albuquerque, or CEO of a company like Chipotle, you should major in Art History like Tim Keller and Steve Ells did.

The point is just the opposite. Your college major does not limit or determine your career options. In fact, your college major is not even the most important factor in determining your career success.

Your passionate approach to the world is far more important. Nurture that passion by studying what you care about. If you can knock it out of the park in Art History, that training will help you tackle even bigger challenges.

That list of executives is crazy

You don't expect me to believe that legendary Southwest Airlines co-founder and CEO Herb Kelleher was an English major.

In addition to majoring in English, Kelleher minored in Philosophy, and then got a degree in Law. But Kelleher's major did not make him a billionaire. Southwest Airlines isn't one of the world's most valuable airlines because Kelleher read Moby Dick, although maybe it helped. What Herb Kelleher really needed was all the different skills like those we talk about in Appendix A – courage, vision, persistence, initiative, empathy, ambiguity tolerance, making hard choices, managing competing priorities, problem-solving, personal discipline, strategic thinking, staying calm under pressure. That's the hidden curriculum of a liberal arts education.

Your brain is still developing, at least until age 25, which makes it somewhat easier to learn new things. College is a great time, and a great place, to make yourself smart in all these important ways. Seize the day. Do not settle for vocational training alone.

Are you against STEM?

Are you suggesting that I avoid STEM?

Not at all! The natural sciences – Astronomy, Biology, Chemistry, Physics, and Mathematics – were founding members of the Liberal Arts curriculum more than 2,000 years ago. Today, these disciplines are at the vanguard of one of the important modes of thinking we'll talk about in Chapter 19, empirical inquiry.[47]

The "T" and the "E" of STEM are slightly different, because they are more closely related to professional or vocational studies.[48]

We favor using a college education for professional or vocational purposes. Indeed, that is one of the five purposes of college, and we have spent a lot of time discussing good ways to do it. There's nothing wrong with being passionate about a major with specific professional potential.

However, we think professional studies like engineering, education, social work, nursing, and business work best when they are added to a Liberal Arts education, not when they replace it.

A good liberal arts education might be one-third general education requirements, one-third major requirements, and one-third electives. If you choose an undergraduate professional program with demanding unit requirements, it will be difficult to achieve breadth in only four years, just as it is difficult when you double-major. And that lack of breadth can cost you later.

Another common problem occurs when students major in some vocationally focused discipline that they do not enjoy because they incorrectly believe that it is required for future employment. Students hear every day that unless they take a narrow vocational approach to their Bachelor's degree, they risk unemployment or low wages. They are also told that they don't have to attend class or learn much – a mere passing grade will entitle them to a privileged spot in the workforce.

Because you are reading this book, know better. You understand how to get flexible job skills that will help you advance in any career, no matter what major you choose. Nurturing your passion and achieving broad, deep understanding is the path to success in all of life's endeavors, including your career.

Unexpected Path

I majored in Zoology because I wanted to be an animal trainer, at an animal park. I got that job, but it paid starvation wages, and I couldn't take it. I ended up doing sales support for a medical device company, which pays well and I enjoy the work. Working with animals, you learn patience, non-verbal communication, and how to help someone adjust to a new situation. Those skills turn out to be extremely relevant to selling. So I wouldn't say that I didn't learn important job skills in college, but they weren't the skills I was expecting or for the job I was expecting.

Chapter 10
Takeaways

- People whose majors are narrowly focused on specific jobs frequently end up in other careers anyway, either because the market changes, their interests change, unexpected opportunities arise, or because competition is stiff

- Often it is less risky to get general skills that will allow you to approach the job market more flexibly

Chapter 11

Homesick in a Strange Land

Well this is disorienting!

You are now living in a strange place with unfamiliar people, likely sharing an apartment kitchen, if not a dormitory bedroom. There may be a dining hall that handles the cooking and the dishes. On-campus residence halls keep a roof over your bed and handle the utilities. There's not much for you to do but eat, sleep, and learn. How does anyone cope with this?

It's one thing to visit for a day; something else to actually move in!

If it's your first time living away from home, then your first challenge may be to put some distance between your new world and your old world. You are making new friends, and accepting new responsibilities, so you need to allow some space to exist between you and your prior world.

For prior generations, this was automatic and involuntary, because when you moved away to college you were pretty much gone. There was no texting, emailing, and social media. Even talking on the phone was once prohibitively expensive. The result was an abrupt, shocking break with the past that led to homesickness and worse.

You can't be serious that students couldn't even phone home.

Today's students have the opposite problem – they can't escape their past, and paradoxically that ALSO often leads to homesickness, because the home they left is never very far away. They are constantly reminded of it.

Homesickness is extremely common. And it is healthy – a measure of the strength of the roots that you set at home. But it is also a sign that you're struggling to build a new community where you are, which is a part of the college task of building your own independent self.

How long does it take to make new friends?

How you respond to homesickness matters. Getting drunk at parties is a bad idea. Talking to counselors about your feelings is a good idea. Earlier we talked about building emotional self-regulation and balance. Learning how to manage your own emotions using healthy outlets is a skill in and out of the classroom.

You will also want to overcome your discomfort and use the college's resources to build a new web of connections. You will need those connections not only to fend off homesickness, but also to support yourself when times get tough and you're unhappy. We'll discuss how to do that in Chapter 15.

In addition to the problem of a new "here" alongside an old "there," students also have the sudden problem of more work with less structure.

People often imagine structure as confining and the lack of structure as liberating, but the truth of the matter is not so simple.

Structure provides support and guidance. We take our cues from our context. If you find yourself in a classroom, you might be inclined to take a seat and focus your attention. If you find yourself in a restaurant, you might be inclined to order some food. But if you find yourself on a college campus, you might do anything, or nothing.

The only really firm structure is that you are supposed to enroll in classes, and the classes require you to do things like listening, speaking, reading, writing, and problem-solving.

But that dooon't toll you how to opond tho root of your time. Should you read more, or write more? Should you go to the library or work out? When have you done enough? It is often not clear.

And even the hard and certain requirements aren't all that hard and certain. How much of the readings do you really have to do, or how carefully do you need to read? How much effort do you need to put into the papers in order to pass? Is merely passing enough? And will they even notice (or care about) your non-attendance? Maybe not, if it's a big lecture hall class.

Do you even have to get out of bed? Nobody is going to come into your room and get you out of bed. Nobody is going to tell you that you have to go to sleep at night. All the choices are yours. This can be difficult.

In Chapter 13 we will discuss how to go about deciding what to do with your time.

College is also an unfamiliar institution. You may be surrounded by characters you have not previously encountered: Chancellors, Provosts, Preceptors, Proctors, Bursars, Resident Assistants, Community Assistants, Adjunct Lecturers, and Department Chairs. Assistant Professors are not Assistants in any respect. You may walk past an "Institute" that has no physical presence besides a sign in somebody's office.

And although the entire system purports to be set up to serve the students, most colleges actually have several other major agendas.

Unless you are trying to get a job on campus, you mostly don't need to know how a university works, or what all those professors are doing when they are not teaching you, and why some faculty do not teach at all.

But the basics about being a university professor are worth knowing, so you can understand a little better your professors and some of the language in the course catalog. Skip to the next chapter if you are not interested in how colleges work or the different kinds of professors.

When a college hires a professor, there are two kinds of positions they might be hired into: tenure-track and non-tenure track.

Tenure-track positions are ones where you can earn "tenure" after a certain number of years. Tenure means your position is permanent as long as you do your job well enough. Specifically, you cannot be fired for the content of your opinions.

Beginning professors who are in tenure track positions but have not yet earned tenure are typically called "Assistant Professors." If tenure is granted, they are promoted to "Associate Professor." Associate Professors who further distinguish themselves may be promoted again to "Full Professor." If the professor retires, they may keep an office and even retain some duties, but they are referred to as "Emeritus" faculty.

When determining whether to grant tenure, universities consider a mix of research, teaching, and service to the institution. But frequently research weighs most heavily in the equation. So Assistant Professors are busy doing research and writing articles about their research to be published in scholarly journals.

If a professor is denied tenure, they are asked to leave the university. The severity of that outcome is what gives rise to the phrase "publish or perish," and it is why Assistant Professors are frequently stressed and harried.

Most professors have a Ph.D. That stands for "Doctor of Philosophy." "Philosophy" in this context includes all kinds of knowledge. This is why professors are often called "Dr."

Non-tenure track positions are usually called "Lecturer." Some lecturers have made a career of it, and may be expected to shoulder a full course load year after year. Lecturers get paid less, and their job is to teach classes that the tenure track faculty aren't available for. If demand requires that a few additional sections of a class be added, there would not be time to do a search for new tenure track faculty, but some lecturers might be available to join the faculty on an interim basis or to teach an additional class. Many lecturers will have Ph.Ds, but some will not.

Undistracted by the requirements of tenure and promotion, lecturers often can devote themselves fully to their teaching duties in ways that tenure-track faculty cannot. But many lecturers also have other jobs that put additional stresses on their time and attention.

In any case, the units and the grade you get from a class are the same regardless of whether it is taught by a professor, a lecturer, or a graduate student.

When shopping for classes, should you prefer full professors to lecturers, or vice versa? Neither. Follow the reviews to detect who will probably deliver the best learning experience.

Thank you! I knew some of that stuff, but not all of it.

Homesickness

So what should I actually do if I am feeling homesick?

Well, don't panic. It's a natural way to feel. So the first thing is to realize that nothing is terribly wrong, besides your unhappiness. You are experiencing something normal that most new college students experience. They got through it, and so will you.

Second, you need to not be tempted by the idea of quitting and going home. That will solve the immediate pain of being homesick, but it will create a new problem, which is that you are stuck at home. Eventually you will have to leave home, and now is a good time to develop that ability.

Third, there are a few things you can do to hasten the transition to living away from home. Think of those feelings of homesickness as a strength – the strength of your affection for family, friends, and place. Value that strength and nurture it. Stay in close touch with your loved ones. Just don't let that affection interfere with the important work you have to do at college.

Fourth, put extra effort into making friends. If you live on campus, keep the door open, and introduce yourself. That way, small talk opportunities later will be easier. If someone invites you to do something, find a way to say yes. Talk to people in your classes; you already have something in common. Join study groups. Go to office hours. Clubs and jobs on campus also can provide many social opportunities.

Making New Friends

First semester is almost over – how long until I make new friends?

It can take time. Your hands are full during your first year, and you may feel overwhelmed. You're just trying to get through it. Often college students make their strongest friendships after first year. By then they know what they like and don't like. Second year is a chance to have another go at it. Unlike in the movies, college friends are not usually the first people you meet on the train to Hogwarts.

Course evaluations

My college experience improved significantly once I started reading the course reviews, which our university made available, although there are also some on the Internet. Before, I had no I idea what to expect from the person at the front. After, I knew not only what to expect, but also that it would match my preferences. I don't want an easy A, I want be challenged, but also supported so that I meet the challenge. A good instructor can make any course interesting. I'd rather take a bad class from a good professor than a good class from a bad professor.

Leaving Home

This is weird, but I ended up having a kind of inverse homesickness. Going home to see friends was great at first, but over time it felt like we had less and less to talk about, and I felt like we started caring about different things. Or maybe it would be more accurate to say that I stopped caring about what they cared about. Eventually I didn't want to go home at all. The loss I started to feel wasn't that I couldn't go back home to see my friends, but that I no longer wanted to. I know that mostly I am the one that changed, and I don't regret anything. But it still makes me sad.

Chapter 11
Takeaways

- College is a strange new place, and feeling homesick is natural and common

- You may need to practice entering unfamiliar situations and making the most of what college offers that you did not have before

- It is important to create structure for your time and decide the best way to spend each day

- Professors, assistant-professors, and adjunct lecturers might all be great instructors

Chapter 12

The Rules You Can't Break

You have done a lot of work to get to college, and by now should be eager to get down to business and make each day great.

But before you can succeed at college, you have to know the rules. There are not that many rules, but they are very important. Each college is likely to have a different version, especially if you are on the quarter system, so figure out what they actually are at your school – it's on the website, and an academic advisor can help -- but basically it goes like this.

Unit requirements. To graduate and get a bachelor's degree, you need to take a certain number of classes, which is measured in units. Typically, a class that meets one hour per week for one semester will count as one unit. A four-unit class will meet for four hours per week . Assuming that your college is on the semester system and requires 120 units[49] to graduate, that would be on average 15 hours of classes per week for eight semesters, or on average four classes per semester.

Breadth requirements. In addition to the total number of classes, you will need to take specific classes that show breadth. These are sometimes referred to as "General Education" or "Breadth" requirements, and you may have to show proficiency in specific disciplines (like language) and/or skills (like writing) and/or areas of study (like global relations). Each college has its own formula, and the formulas tend to change, so you need to determine the rules in effect for you.

Major requirements. Beyond that, you will also have to satisfy the requirements of one major. Each major sets its own rules, but typically there will be some specific classes required for everyone in the major, and then you may have some flexibility with additional courses (e.g., one from this group and two from that group). Majors often require a final project, such as a thesis, presentation, or portfolio.

To graduate, you will need to satisfy all of the requirements for graduation. Do not show up on the last day having completed your breadth and major requirements but not your unit requirements, and expect to get a degree. It is your job to know the degree requirements and to satisfy all of them. If your advisor told you wrong, or you misunderstood, then you don't graduate. The college can't waive these rules. They are required by accrediting institutions. So make sure you have this right.

What if one class satisfies two requirements?

Minimum Grades. Most schools will throw you out if you don't maintain a minimum grade level, typically C or above. If you're not serious about learning, then they will give your spot to someone who is. Before they throw you out, though, you'll find yourself on "academic warning," and then "academic probation," so it wouldn't come as a surprise, and you will have a chance to fix it.

Cheating. Another important rule is no cheating. We know from experience that students now and then get themselves into a tight spot where they are unable to complete an assignment at the desired quality level within the allotted time.

So they decide to cheat.

But doesn't everyone do it? And doesn't that mean I'm a sucker if I don't?

There are lots of ways to cheat, but they mostly come down to having another person or machine do the work for you.

There's no better, faster way to destroy your college education than to cheat.

That's only partly because you will most likely get caught, and the penalties are severe – they'll throw you out.

The reason you will get caught is because colleges can't exist if students cheat. The college's credentialing function becomes meaningless if someone can get the degree without getting the learning. Because cheating is an existential threat to colleges, they put a lot of resources into catching and expelling cheaters.

Colleges have spent way more time thinking about it than you have, and they have purchased expensive technology to monitor it. The professors have all had experience with cheaters, and they often are skilled at detecting cheating.

The risk involved with cheating is very high – high risk of getting caught, and significant penalty if caught.

The benefits of cheating, by contrast, are small. If you are otherwise doing good work in a class, turning in one paper that is late or subpar won't hurt you much. And if you are otherwise doing bad work in a class, rescuing one paper won't help you much.

If a single assignment is the difference between a barely passing grade and a failing grade, then there still isn't much to be gained by getting credit for barely passing a class that in fact you did not pass. But if you have to cheat repeatedly to pass classes, then the risk of your getting caught is really high.

The risk of getting caught ought to be enough to dissuade most cheaters, but it is not.

So we would draw your attention to another loss, at least as grave, and that is your integrity. One of the reasons you are going to college is to learn who you are. That sense of identity will ground you and guide you for the rest of your life. What a sad disappointment it would be to discover that you are the kind of person who cheats?

The reason that discovery is disappointing is because cheating hurts everyone else in the class. You were never the only one who ran out of time. You were never the only one who couldn't figure out how to do a great job. But those other people either put in their best effort and found a way, or they did work that was subpar or late and accepted the consequences of their actions.

That accepting of the consequences is the big win. It is how you learn to navigate the difficulties of life, which very frequently serve up no-win situations and impossible compromises.

Learning to make tradeoffs and to live with the consequences of those tradeoffs is one of the things college has to teach you. And if you understand that deeply enough, you may be motivated to and able to plan in advance, often in ways that will prevent you from getting into the bad situation in the first place.

Cheating in a class is no different from stealing from the store what others had to pay for. It may feel different, but it is not.

So here is how to not cheat.

How to NOT cheat?
Who needs to know
how NOT to cheat?

First, allow yourself to feel the urge to cheat. It comes on as fear, and then panic. You're afraid to be seen as a failure by others. You're afraid to see yourself as a failure. You're afraid that if you do badly on the assignment things will spiral out of control – a bad grade on the assignment will lead to a bad grade in the course will lead to your eventually being unemployed, homeless, and alone in the world.

Feel all that fear, recognize it for what it is – irrational, self-destructive panic – and then just accept the consequences of your having gotten yourself into this situation, and move on.

The sun will come up tomorrow. And when it does, it will shine upon someone with personal integrity, who sometimes makes ill-advised decisions or misjudges things, but who accepts the consequences of their actions, and gets smarter, stronger, and better each day.

Each time you resist the urge to cheat you actually become a better version of yourself.

GEs

I've heard of GE requirements. Those are the things we want to get out of the way so we can graduate, right?

Omg. GE requirements are the best part. They are one of the main purposes. It's your big chance to learn all the things they didn't teach you in high school, like Philosophy, Sociology, Anthropology, Psychology, Communication, Geology, Environmental Studies, Theater, French Literature, Design, Art History, and dozens of others. Relish it! Make the most of it! It's so important, that it is the only universal requirement in college.

Units

Why won't the college waive the unit requirement if I am one unit short and it wasn't my fault?

Outside accrediting agencies audit colleges regularly to confirm that the colleges are meeting their standards, including minimum requirements to graduate. The college needs the accreditation to establish its legitimacy and to retain funding sources. So the college cannot easily or casually depart from the accreditation requirements without putting the institution at risk.

Cheating

If I know that other students are cheating, that makes me feel like I need to as well, just for things to be fair, uh, if you know what I mean…

If college teaches you anything, let it be not to take foolish risks just because others are being foolish. Remember: cheating just once won't make a big difference for your overall performance, and cheating regularly will certainly lead to your getting caught. Colleges have much more experience detecting cheaters than you have trying not be detected, and they have every incentive to detect cheating. And even if you were not confronted, there could be consequences that you are unaware of.

But most important, discovering in yourself the person who has too much integrity to cheat, and has enough ego strength to accept the consequences of their actions – that is a treasure that will prove its worth over and over again, long after you have left college behind.

Minor Cheating

What about little tiny cheats that won't get me thrown out, like using Google Translate in language class?

Don't do it. Even if they don't throw you out, they're still likely to notice. And they will think worse of you for it, even if they don't tell you. That hurts your relationships, and your chance to get letters of recommendation. It costs you the learning you would have gotten if you'd done the work. And your integrity takes a big hit for at most a very small benefit.

Academic Warning

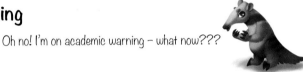

Oh no! I'm on academic warning – what now???

Don't panic. Talk to your advisor. They will tell you what it means, and what you need to do. You also have to figure out what's stopping you from performing well. Are you partying too much, or working too much? Do you have reasonable expectations about what college requires? Are you taking courses you hate because you think you have to? There is a lot to consider. But you can solve it, if you want to. This is a learning experience. Make the most of it.

Why I cheated

I didn't want to cheat; I didn't plan to cheat. I felt like I had to cheat. I just couldn't face failing – the embarrassment in the eyes of others, and the shame in my own eyes. I don't know how they knew, but when I was confronted I burst into tears. Then I was really in trouble, and I could not imagine why getting a lower grade or points taken off for lateness seemed so scary, when what I ended up facing was so much worse.

Short on units

I ended up one unit shy for graduation, which at my college meant 119 units instead of 120. I figured there was no way the college would make me enroll in another semester for $10,000 to get one unit, especially since they wanted me to graduate on time more than I did. What I didn't realize was that letting me graduate with 119 units was against a law. They didn't have any choice. But I ended up getting the extra unit in summer session, which wasn't that bad. And I actually really loved that last class I took!

Chapter 12
Takeaways

- You need to know the rules, especially the graduation requirements. They normally can't be waived

- The temptation to cheat can be overwhelming, but it's always a bad idea. The urge to cheat is a natural response to panic and stress, but there is a better way to deal with it than giving in to the urge

- Let yourself feel the panic. But then calm down and re-read Chapter 12 so you know what to do instead, and why

Chapter 13

Managing Priorities

There is a lot to learn, and not much time. Four years will be gone before you know it. You're going to be very busy.

So to get this right, you will need a lot of personal management skills. Do you keep a calendar? You need to keep a calendar. Do you use a daily planner? You need to use a daily planner. Are you self-motivated? You need to be self-motivated.

In this chapter we are only going to touch on personal effectiveness at the highest level. There are whole books on this that go deep into the topic, and you should spend time with such books if you have not already.

Also check your college's academic support services (sometimes called "Learning Center" or "Writing Center"). They'll have tips on the latest software and productivity apps to help you get organized and stay focused.

Self-motivation

Why do we do anything? Why do we even get out of bed? It's because there is something else we care about more than staying in bed, and we have to get up and do something for it to happen.

Personal motivation is about correctly understanding what we care about, and deciding to act to make it happen.

It's easy to start keeping a daily planner, but to keep using it for more than a week takes more discipline than I have. I can go ten days max, then I drop it.

Such as...?

That's easier said than done. You should spend a good deal of time by yourself in contemplation weighing all the things you want (wealth, fame, respect, love, power, friends, a partner, children, a pet, a feeling of belonging, etc.), with the costs of those things, and understanding the difficult trade-offs involved.

Some people start with the end in mind, imagining what they would like written on their tombstone, and who they would want to attend their funeral, and what things they would like said. Then they work backward from that to engineer a life in which things are more likely to resolve that way.

Or maybe you don't know everything you want, but you know one thing for sure, and are willing to anchor your plans around that thing.

However you approach it, you have to know where you are trying to go or you won't get there.

Imagine that your only goal is to make each day the very best day that it can be. So you wake up with no long-term plans at all, and live only to discover the opportunity of the present moment.

Could be fun.

Behold the complete and perfect is-ness of this moment!

But don't imagine that that isn't a long-range plan. It is a plan – a plan to not care about what happens in the future – to not anticipate, to not prepare, to not plan, but only to have your plans constrained by outside forces.

But what if, when you arrive in the future, things aren't to your liking, and you realize that you DID care about what happens, and you are really sorry that you didn't direct things more closely toward what you valued, because now some of what might have been possible no longer is?

The problem, of course, is who knows what we will want in the future? We can have some confidence in what we want for ourselves right now, but how can we reliably guess what our future self 10, 20, or 50 years from now will wish that we had done, or what our future family members might wish for us when they don't yet even exist?

We cannot. And yet, our ignorance does not make the question go away. And to ignore the question is to let others decide our future.

One reasonable approach is to keep options open. If I can't rule out the possibility that I might want to become a doctor, I might take some pre-med courses just in case.

That works for a while. And that is exactly what you are doing when you enter college with your major undeclared – you don't have enough information to decide yet.

But you can't keep all the options open indefinitely; each of those just-in-case choices has costs. So eventually you have to decide.

You don't have to decide today. But you do have to decide. Not deciding ever is itself a decision with significant consequences.

So devote serious time to this; plus, ideally, a little time each week to adjust and refine your course.

To Do Lists

Suppose you set for yourself these three goals. You at least know for sure that you want: (1) To learn as much as you can during your college years, (2) To have a good circle of friends, and

(3) To find your calling that makes the world a better place, and/or brings you joy and fulfillment

Now you have charted a course. The next step is to create a to-do list.

Always use to-do lists. Get an electronic to-do list, and make sure it automatically syncs between as many devices as you have, so no matter where you are, no matter what you are looking at, you can always, easily, add to-do items or check them off.

Put everything on your to-do lists. People you need to talk to, movies you need to watch, questions you need to ask, things you need to buy, everything. Human minds are not optimized for holding on to large lists. If you think you will remember everything, you will almost certainly be mistaken.

But even if you occasionally manage to remember everything, that success will have taken a great deal of unnecessary sustained concentration. You should free up your mind for better things. Get all those lists written down so your mind doesn't have to worry about any of that and can go back to thinking great thoughts.

Keeping a Calendar.

Your calendar is a subset of your to-do lists. It is just the items that have a date or a time associated with them. Typically these will be meetings or events, but it could be anything with a deadline: paper due by X date, or tickets go on sale starting on Y date, or a visitor is coming on Z date so you have to perform some tasks in preparation for that.

Your calendar should be electronic so it can send you alerts about what you are supposed to be doing, when, and where. If you don't have an electronic calendar keeping track of all that for

The last time I tried a to-do list it filled with so many to-dos that one to-do become more important than all the others: Throw out the to-do list!

you, then you will have to use your brain to keep track of it, and your brain can only handle so many things at once. So to optimize college learning, take any unnecessary load off your brain. A calendar is necessary for that.

But the calendar doesn't only make thinking easier. It will help you to not make mistakes.

Your success in most endeavors depends in part upon whether others trust you. They will trust you if you make and keep commitments. The calendar will help you do that.

By contrast, if you miss deadlines and skip meetings, people will think you are disorganized. They might even think you are flaky. They won't trust you as much, and you will have fewer opportunities. Are they right? Do we call people unreliable simply because they do not use their calendar well? Or do people not use their calendar well if they are in fact unreliable?

Use your calendar well.

Avoiding Over-programming

If you put everything on your to-do lists, as we have suggested, then soon there will be too many things to do, and you may feel overwhelmed. When that happens, you are over-programmed.

How do you avoid getting too many things on your to-do list?

That's what I said!

There are three reasons why an item gets on your to-do list even though it should not be there.

First, you might overly describe an item. Going downstairs could be one task, or each step on the staircase could be its own task. Better to just identify the task at the highest level of generality that will remind you what to do: "Empty trash" contains within it all the necessary subtasks, whether it involves going downstairs, putting on shoes, gathering the trash items, or whatever.

Second, you might include a low-priority item that isn't ever going to get done. These aspirational tasks will plug up your to-do lists until they no longer matter, or until you admit that it's just not going to happen. If admitting it isn't going to happen is too psychologically painful still, simply create a list called "Some Day" or "Eventually" and they can sit there out of the way, causing no harm, indefinitely. And who knows, maybe one day you will eventually check that list.

Third, there may be a task that does not serve an important purpose. Every task on your list should be in service of some greater goal that you are trying to accomplish. If not, then don't do it. It's using up time that could be spent on things that matter.

Earlier, we said that the only three goals we identified were:

1. To learn as much as we could during our college years,

2. To have a good circle of friends, and

3. To work toward a career that makes the world a better place.

So suppose you notice some task on your list like "Go to the store for milk." That does not support any of your three goals, even indirectly, so you can either remove the task from your list as unimportant, or realize that your list of just three goals is actually incomplete.

It turns out that there is something else we care about, too. Maybe it's "Being Healthy," or "Running the Household," or "Cooking at Home." Add that to the list of goals, because we are going to do it, and it is going to use up time and energy. It must be accounted for in our goals.

You do not want to be in a position where you don't achieve your three goals because those weren't really your goals. You had a bunch of other goals that were silent, secret, or unstated, but still manifesting in your task list, and possibly deprioritizing what you thought were the most important things.

So now add those to your goal list.

You can learn a lot about your real goals just by watching your actual behavior. If you say your goal is to do well in school, but the way you actually spend your time is watching movies, going to parties, playing video games, and surfing, then doing well in school might not actually be a goal. At the very least, it is not a high priority goal. Your high priority goal might be something like "Having Fun," or "Spending Time with Friends."

There is nothing wrong with having fun or spending time with your friends. You are free to make those your highest priority goals, too. The only thing we advise is that you write down that that is what you are doing, so each day it can be a conscious choice. And then if your goals change, you can adjust your activities accordingly.

Incidentally, it can go the other way, too. You tell yourself that your highest goal is to build strong interpersonal relationships and spend time with family, but then observe that your task list is filled with school and work tasks, to the serious detriment of your interpersonal affairs. That doesn't mean you have to change your activities. You might just need to reassess what really are your goals.

In fact, you should think about your tasks and your goals every day and make minor corrections on a regular basis, rather than steering between occasional life-shocking epiphanies that you are doing everything wrong.

There is room for a bit of everything, but you have to make that room by balancing your priorities. To balance your priorities, you first need to know what they are. You determine what they are by watching your behavior and then consciously deciding whether that matches what is in your heart.

The power of a system like this is that by aligning your actions with your goals, you harness your emotional energy (what you care about) to power your physical energy (what you do), which can get your life moving remarkably fast in exactly the direction you want.

The risk of a system like this is that after a week you forget why you are doing it, you stop doing it, and you fall back into old habits. Then your daily tasks fall out of alignment with your most deeply felt goals and values, and your days become rudderless.

There are lots of ways to manage tasks, so don't be afraid to try new strategies. And remember, other students, and maybe even faculty, are also figuring this out. Ask others for their strategies and what tools they use to get some ideas of where to start.

Consulting your values and goals every day, and your progress toward those goals every week, and making sure your stated goals are really your goals, can keep you on track and prevent you from losing steam.

Identifying priorities

So which actually is it: Do I decide my priorities and then conform my actions, or do I watch my actions and infer my priorities?

Could be either. They are not mutually inconsistent. Which works better for you? Some people are more consciously aware of what motivates them and like to plan and strategize; others need to feel their way through.

I will say this, though: Students often come to me with problems and tell me what they care about most, and there is a significant mismatch between what they say they care about and what they actually do. Those two things must come into alignment.

Personal effectiveness

You said there were good books on personal effectiveness – any recommendations?

There is quite a bit written on the topic. Stephen Covey's "The Seven Habits of Highly Effective People" is a classic, and certainly worth your time. Look into bullet journaling, and FranklinCovey® planners. Ask among your friends, colleagues, faculty, and the staff at your college's Learning Center to find titles and materials that might particularly speak to you.

Avoiding over-programming

Any tricks to avoid over-programming myself?

Just recognize you're doing it, and manage it. There are only 24 hours in a day. Nothing can change that, so if you give yourself more tasks than you can do, you are being unrealistic, and possibly demoralizing yourself. There may be a way to improve your capabilities so that you can do 25% more things in a day, but you will still only be able to do as much as you can do, so use the "Some Day" list to keep track of things that are not priorities right now, but might become priorities later.

It's worth mentioning that sometimes what seems like over-programming isn't actually over-programming, but over-consumption of social media or otherwise getting lost in time-sucks.

Too much productivity?

Don't tell me about productivity! I use to-do lists to make to-do lists, and color-coded calendars, so I can do three times what other students do, including a triple-major!

Congratulations on discovering the productivity tools. You can see how powerful they are. But the tools need to be servants, not masters. Productivity for the sake of appearing productive to others, or to yourself, is not the big win. The big win is first determining what you value most, and then making sure that you are efficiently and effectively accomplishing that. A triple-major, for example, is trying to prove something, not to accomplish something.

Motivation

I just can't get motivated.

If you literally cannot get out of bed or do anything, then you may have depression and should talk to the counseling service.

But if you can find the motivation to do some things, like play games, have fun, watch movies, and socialize, but you can't get motivated to do difficult things like studying and learning, then the problem isn't that you lack motivation, but that you aren't motivated about the right things -- you don't believe in your heart that studying and learning are necessary for you to get what you really do want.

Only you can decide. But make sure you are very clear about what you want to happen in your life, and what it will take to get there. You might find your motivation comes on strong when you have clarity about those things.

Time management

Time management is everything. Everyone gets the same number of hours per day, and what happens to you depends on how you use them. How you use them depends on what you decide to do. And what you decide to do depends on what you care about. I can't say I spend every hour of every day doing the thing I should most be doing. But it helps me a lot to think about it every day – that way I can get close to the target even on days when I don't hit it.

Socializing for work

Socializing is never far from the top of my to-do list. There are all kinds of jobs that require first-rate social skills, from communications manager to Hollywood agent to cruise ship director. People are social and the work world thrives on connections. College is where I made mine.

Chapter 13

Takeaways

- Keep a to-do list, and put everything on it

- Keep a calendar to help you meet your commitments to others

- Know your values and goals to make sure that your to-do list isn't filled with things that don't deserve to be there

- Avoid over-programming by using a "some day" list to store items that you care about but are currently lower priority

Chapter 14

Learning Outside Your Classes

Now that you know why you are in college, you have the tools, you know the rules, you know the habits you need to develop, and you are proactively arranging your tasks and ensuring that they advance your goals, you are finally ready to begin learning.

So how does that happen?

You are going to be spending a lot of time reading and in classrooms.

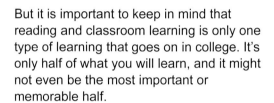

But it is important to keep in mind that reading and classroom learning is only one type of learning that goes on in college. It's only half of what you will learn, and it might not even be the most important or memorable half.

We are not saying that your classes are not important, or that you should not take your classes seriously. On the contrary, the materials you are covering are very important, and the mental practices involved in learning them – like painting and waxing in *The Karate Kid* – will serve you for your entire life.

Nonetheless, you will get far less than a complete education if you neglect the activities outside the classroom, including student life, student government, residential life, clubs, theater, events, activities, guest lectures, debates, poetry readings, concerts, athletics, internships, job-shadowing, undergraduate publications, and everything else that makes colleges and universities such vibrant communities.

You can learn a lot from books. Indeed, much of the knowledge and wisdom accumulated throughout history has been recorded in books.

But people naturally learn by doing. And much of what you are going to learn involves not what things were like in the past, but what you are like right now. You need to practice interacting with people in new ways, and in new contexts, and begin to exercise leadership skills.

You will encounter conflicts over campus issues. Students sometimes get upset about the expansion or contraction of student services, changes to university policies, or something as simple as whether beloved trees get removed to make room for campus growth.

You will likely encounter heated emotions and frothy argument. Observe how you react to that. Observe how others react. How do different people approach problems differently? Do you see people from different backgrounds navigating the situation differently? Are people able to effectively express their own views and also understand competing views? How do we collectively find our way to peaceful resolution on matters of acute disagreement? Which approaches work better? If our side does not prevail, how should we respond?

Social conflicts are a permanent part of human affairs, and anyone running anything will encounter them frequently. Deepen your understanding by engaging with others. Maybe the tree survives, or maybe the tree gets the axe. But you can win either way if you improve your ability to engage constructively in such conflicts.

I'm for the tree!

It's just a tree, you idiot!

Now you listen here!

Emotional self-regulation is one of the skills to be mastered, and there is no better way to discover whether your propensity is to be even-keeled, or instead to over- or under-react, than by engaging with others over the hotly debated issues of the day. You may be a born fighter or conflict-averse. Neither of those is intrinsically good or bad. But you need to be able to manage and modulate your reactivity to your emotional state in order to think clearly and act effectively.

Of course it does not all have to be about conflict. People can come together constructively to do something interesting, important, or difficult, even if there is no opposition at all. That likely will involve a good deal of coordination and planning, including a big-picture orientation about what the group is trying to accomplish (strategy), and a detail orientation to make sure each necessary step is done well (execution).

Like starting an "Old Movies" club!

I don't like old movies!

Have you ever seen one?

You will learn, too, about money. Everything in the world has a budget. With unlimited resources, we could do unlimited things. But almost always the challenge is to accomplish objectives with limited resources. And often if the thing cannot be done inexpensively, then it will not be done at all. This requires creativity, compromise and problem-solving – again, real-world skills that you will use for the rest of your life. You can discuss and simulate in classrooms in theory, but you will learn even more when you practice in real life as you participate in campus affairs.

Without a budget, our old movies club can't show any old movies...

So this is where you practice taking initiative: join a club, write for the student paper, listen to a speech, attend a protest, play for a team, and join with others to make something better. Watch for flyers for campus programming. The principles you learn in the classroom will give you a deeper theoretical understanding of the human condition. But to complete your learning you must put theory into practice.

We'll talk more about grades in in Chapter 25, but notice now that these extra-curricular activities – participation in clubs, activities, internships, theater, student journalism, residential life, student government, or other campus activities – are typically ungraded. Yet they are still incredibly important. You will learn skills that you will use for the rest of your life – collaboration, problem-solving, creativity, negotiation, determination, communication, building trust, and more. You won't be graded, but you will still learn.

Oh yeah!

How will you prove that you learned what you were supposed to learn by participating in campus life if you don't have a grade? The same way you will prove all the other skills you picked up in courses that were graded: by demonstrating them.

Some students fantasize that a future employer will be impressed by their degree and will give them a lot of money. It doesn't work that way at all.

The only thing that dazzles employers is your ability to solve problems and deliver results in whatever position you have been entrusted with. The degree may be enough to give you a chance to prove it – which is great! It's what we want! – but if you can't deliver, your career will stall or crash.

That actually makes sense.

So if you have learned what you are supposed to learn, you will have a chance to demonstrate it. In fact, you will have to.

On the other hand, if you spend all of your college years in class and in books, and you did not take any time to participate in the wealth of outside-the-classroom educational opportunities on campus, prospective employers may look sideways at your application. If you did not engage with others in activities designed to accomplish something in the real world, if you do not attend theater or museum exhibits or enrich yourself in any way other than sitting in a library, prospective future employers may doubt that you picked up enough non-intellectual skills, or that you have the curiosity and self-direction necessary to do complex or challenging work.

Job interviewers routinely ask what you did at college besides study. They aren't looking for particular items. They want to hear who you are, what you care about, how you make a difference, and how you will perform when things get difficult in real-life ways.

Whether you are captain of the badminton team or you started a society for creative anachronism does not matter. It's the act of leading something or starting something or caring about something – and following through – that they want to hear about.

Think of it like pole-vaulting. If you want to learn to pole vault, you can read about how to pole-vault, but most of your pole-vaulting education will come from actually practicing with a pole. That part is essential.

Anyone who only attends classes and is not otherwise engaged with the college community is missing out on a big part of the education. Getting good grades cannot make up for it. Which is another reason not to overemphasize grades, in addition to the considerations in Chapter 25.

Unusual activities

Badminton captain?

Responsibility. Initiative. Problem solving. Teamwork. Communication. Staying calm under pressure. Commitment. Which sport or activity doesn't matter much, in the same way that which major doesn't matter much.

Internships

I don't really want to learn anything in the classroom that I don't apply in real life, so the college's internship office (in the Career Center, where I went) was my best friend. I always had some kind of outside work going in parallel with my classes, and most of what I was learning I put to use. In retrospect, it wasn't just the internships that made that work, because I also put my learning to use in social situations and with my family. But maybe the internships made it more obvious to me that the theory we were studying did in fact have practical applications.

Learning About Organizations

I did great in my college classes, but the most important lessons I learned were from participating in student government. I realized quickly that I didn't know how to be in student government – I didn't understand what was going on, or who was empowered to do what or not – or even how to exercise influence over those who did have power. I had to quickly figure out what was possible and what was not possible, and how things happened or didn't happen. Of course, throughout life I have since found myself in similar situations – needing to get something done in an unfamiliar organization. I was never in student government again, but it was essentially the same situation, and I had an advantage over others, because I had a lot of practice and a few failures under my belt.

Balancing classroom learning

I treated classes as the least important part of my college education. I was active in student politics, attended protests, organized rallies, and was always exhausted, but happy. In retrospect, though, it's possible that I overdid it. What seemed like important accomplishments did not last. I built some skills in myself that lasted, like courage, independence, and public speaking, but I probably missed a lot by not being present for classes, and, honestly, I don't even know what.

Chapter 14
Takeaways

- College isn't just about books and classes; all that learning has to be applied outside the classroom to make it real

- People naturally learn by doing. To complete your learning, you must put theory into practice

- Employers don't care as much about GPA as many students think; they also need to know how well you function in the real world. That's one reason they will ask about your extra-curricular activities

Chapter 15

Finding Your Community

There is a lot to do at college – a lot to keep track of, a lot to fit in, and a lot of complexity.

Help yourself by (1) taking care of yourself, and (2) building a support system: a team of friends and mentors who can help you when things get difficult, as they sometimes will.

Start with yourself. Self-soothing is when you do things to calm yourself in the moment, like eating ice cream, stretching, running, or meditation. Self-soothing gets you through difficult moments, but provides no lasting benefit.

Self-care is when you strengthen yourself for the long-term, like working out, eating well, sleeping enough, going to therapy, using time management techniques, and developing study strategies. Self-care continually strengthens your ability to handle greater and greater challenges.

Also, you should build a supportive community. If you are not a naturally social person, it may feel difficult to build those connections. You will need to go outside your comfort zone and engage with people socially and allow acquaintances to develop. Some of those acquaintances will turn into friendships.

Residential life on college is set up to help you.

You already have something in common with the people in your classes. You also have something in common with the people in your residence. Start there.

And if you don't live on campus, there are still lots of ways to connect with others. Student fees pay for clubs and activities that will bring you together with others. There might be hundreds of student organizations at your college: playing chess, rowing dragon boats, public interest research, a cappella singing, Brazilian Jiu-jitsu, Chinese calligraphy, dog lovers, hiking, biking, improv, LARPing, African dance.

Someone has already made a club for whatever political, cultural, intellectual, or peculiar interest you might have, or you can start one yourself. Need to buy flying discs for your flying disc club? Student government might fund things like that.

You can also join student government. There are all kinds of committees that need members. Find out how things are run, and why, and meet other people interested in that.

You might find your home base in a group that matches your ethnic, cultural, or sexual identity, or that reflects your aspirations or ideals.

But you'll have to push past your discomfort and put yourself in a position to meet other people, and to talk with them – at first about nothing, and then about something.

The whole point of colleges having hundreds of clubs and residential life programs and office hours and academic advising offices and welcome week and weekly events is to give you spaces where you can go talk and connect with people. So pick one, or pick all of them, until you find one where you can sort of jibe with people.

Help yourself, too, by steering clear of the familiar, known, and proven temptations and distractions that are likely to derail your efforts.

We talked earlier about the fountain of knowledge being located near other magical fountains in the forest -- the fountains of drinking, partying, video games, greek life, streaming entertainment, social media, sexual exploration, and trivia. Any of these may be good in small doses, but any of them can also become encompassing obsessions, and swallow up far more of your time and energy than they deserve – to the detriment of your most deeply held values and goals.

You need to understand your susceptibility to such temptations, and take appropriate precautions.

I was supposed to have written those goals down, wasn't I?

Again, we are not suggesting that any of these activities is intrinsically bad. Indeed, each one contains within it some intrinsically good elements, and is also tied to some externally good elements. For example, playing video games can be both social and educational (depending on the game).

How can I know if other activities are costing me my values and goals if I don't know what my values and goals even are?

The measure is always your values and life goals, and whether these engaging activities are advancing them a little, advancing them a lot, or holding you back. If they are advancing you a little, but something else could be advancing you more, then you need to check whether you are over-investing in that activity in a way that gives you pleasure in the short run but will decrease your life satisfaction in the long run.

You should engage in the kind of self-care that improves your self-control and emotional balance so that when unexpected troubles hit you have both the internal and external resources to weather the storm and hold to your course.

How much self-care

I plan to fully support myself by doing as little work as possible and relaxing as much as possible – that will improve both my physical and mental health!

Nice try. By "support yourself," we mean to maximize your ability to do good work, not to maximize your enjoyment or relaxation.

Remember, there is important work to be done at college, and every minute you spend indulging some appetite is time away from something important.

This chapter is a caution not to over-exert yourself. College learning is hard work, and if you exhaust yourself, stress-yourself, or sleep-deprive yourself, you won't do your best work. So take as much time off as you need, but do not take more time off than you need.

Partying as self-care

So partying is good because it helps me learn better?

IF partying helps you learn better, then it might be useful. But be careful how you "relax." Many things that people think of as relaxing are actually exhausting – that includes sunbathing and drinking alcohol, both of which stress your metabolism. Even watching a movie can drain you emotionally and intellectually, if the material is sufficiently challenging or upsetting.

Doing too much

If I learned anything in college, it's that if you don't take time for yourself, you won't have time for anything else, either. And I learned it the hard way. I tried to do everything, and ended up a nervous wreck, accomplishing nothing.

Doing too little

I have so many friends who are self-care experts. They get massages, they meditate, they work for a minute then rest for an hour. They don't get anything done. And then they look at me and they can't believe how much I can fit in. How do you know how much time to take for yourself, and how much to devote to what you're doing? I don't know the best way. What I do is work toward my goals until I'm too tired and can't focus. Then I rest until I can focus again.

Chapter 15

Takeaways

- Build a support system: a team of friends and mentors whom you can talk to when things get difficult

- Keep things from getting too difficult by avoiding temptations and distractions that might put you in a bad spot later

- Take as much time off as you need to support your productivity and effectiveness, but do not take more time off than you need

Chapter 16

Getting Help

College isn't easy if you do it right; you kind of want to make it as difficult as you can. Stretching yourself is good.

If you do the opposite, and make it as easy as you can, that's the same as going to the gym and lifting one-pound weights or using the treadmill for just 90 seconds: total waste of gym membership fee (or tuition).

But, like at the gym, it's easy to overdo it. At college, that occurs when you overcommit yourself. A class is more difficult than you expected, or an activity requires more than you planned for, and everything is too expensive, so you save money in ways that cost you time that you do not have.

And going to college is a big transition. If the admissions office has done its work well, you will be surrounded by a diverse collection of students demonstrating cultural norms that might be new to you. And these new colleagues might be intellectually advanced, ready to challenge your thinking. It might be great fun, but it might be disorienting. You might experience imposter syndrome. You might feel homesick. You might worry about mental or emotional exhaustion. You could get seriously stressed.

Don't panic. Almost everyone suffers some transition shock and confusion at college. The key is to get help. Because they know

What if I stretch out right here and make college as easy as I can?

that many, many students need it, the college is ready for you.

There is **admissions advising.** Admissions advisors will help you apply in the first place. And if you have to withdraw, they can help with that, and then they can help you come back.

There is **academic advising.** Academic advisors will help you navigate the academic program's various requirements, from how to get registered on the first day, to how to confirm that you have met the graduation requirements on the last day, and everything class-related in between.

There is **residential advising.** If you are having trouble with housing on campus – either getting it or keeping it or interacting with others living on campus, or if you want to make the residential life experience even better, residential advisors are there to help. They may be called Resident Assistants, Preceptors, Peer Advisors, or Community Advisors, and they can help you navigate those kinds of problems. If the college has a housing office, they may be able to help you find housing off-campus as well as on-campus.

There are **learning advisors**, too – tutors who can help you with math, writing, and other subjects. Visiting the Writing Center is an especially good idea. Everyone's writing can be improved, but you need another pair of eyes for that to happen, and some expert tips.

Isn't "research" just Googling?

There are **research advisors** – that's the library. Librarians will teach you how to do research, and they can help you with your assignments. They can find resources that you don't know exist and that are much better than Wikipedia. And they understand the citation style rules. If you don't know who to ask, ask a librarian.

There is **financial aid advising.** Paying for college can be a huge challenge. There are many opportunities for loans and scholarships, but they all have different rules and application processes. The Financial Aid Office can help you figure out the right thing to do for your situation.

There is **career advising.** Although your college courses and choice of majors are typically not specific to any particular vocation, you can still plan for your post-college employment far in advance. If your career aspirations require additional credentials, like graduate or professional programs or vocational certificates, the career office can help you get into those programs. Job shadowing opportunities can give you a more realistic sense of what a career you are considering might really be like. The career office also knows about internships and summer jobs that can help you practice applying your new college skills in the work world.

There is **disability counseling.** If you have a disability that requires an accommodation, the Disabilities Office can help you to understand what is possible, and they can communicate with your instructors. The Disabilities Office can help you even with temporary disabilities, like a broken limb that would require assistance taking notes or getting to class. Although disability accommodations cannot modify or diminish the academic requirements, they can ensure that the class format is adjusted to meet your needs.

Your campus may also have a **cultural center**, which offers an additional opportunity to connect with other students. The cultural center will know about groups, clubs, programs, and events of special interest to students with your background and experience, and it can help you find supportive communities at college.

There is also **psychological counseling.** Stress, depression, and the feeling of being overwhelmed can prevent you from functioning at your best, or sometimes even functioning at all. In extreme cases, students may have trouble getting out of bed, or may experience suicidal thoughts. If you believe that stress, anxiety, or depression may be interfering with your ability to do your best work at college, contact the psychological counseling service at once. If they can't meet with you immediately, that shows that other students are having a similar experience. You are not alone, and there is help to get you through.

And for some situations, you may need to talk to multiple advisors. For example, if you think you ended up at the wrong college – that this one isn't working out the way you had hoped – you might want to talk to an Academic Advisor, a Financial Aid Advisor, an Admissions Advisor, a Residential Advisor, and/or a Psychological Counselor.

Every kind of help

Why is so much help available?

First, the college wants you succeed. They don't want you to drop out. So every kind of help you need is provided. They can't do the work for you, but they can remove barriers to your success. You can do it!

Second, they process thousands and thousands of students, so they have seen every kind of problem, and they are ready for it. Tell them about yours. Don't hide it. Whatever your issue is, you are not the first. There is help to get you through, and when you get to the other side, you will be glad you did, and stronger because of it.

Depression

Not gonna lie, I went to college and went right into a depression. Nearly failed out my first quarter, just from not going to classes. And not because I had something better to do. My expectations for college were all wrong, and I wasn't really ready to leave home. I didn't have to summon a bunch of courage to go to the counseling office; several people convinced me, and thank god they did. Long story short, I got my act together and even became a leader on campus. It wasn't even that hard. I had psyched myself out. My worst enemy was me.

Chapter 16
Takeaways

- College is difficult. Almost everyone suffers some transition shock and confusion at college. The key is to get help when you need it

- Familiarize yourself with all the kinds of advising that are available – academic, admissions, career, disability, financial aid, learning, social, emotional, research, residential – and use it when you need it

Part 4

College-Level Work

Chapter 17

How to Read

You must think that you learned how to read a long time ago, but you probably have not learned enough.

Did you know that in 1940 Mortimer Adler wrote a book called *"How to Read a Book?"* that was a million-copy best-seller translated into multiple languages? Decades later, in 1972, a revised and expanded edition was issued. It is 350 pages long.

WTH? You couldn't understand the book unless you already knew how to read!

By definition, everyone who read, *"How to Read a Book"* already knew how to read a book. And yet they needed to learn more. So do you.

That's because you are going to encounter a lot of texts in college, and different kinds of texts, too. If you can read those more effectively, more efficiently, more insightfully – you will learn more, faster, and better.

Did you know that you should read fiction and non-fiction totally differently?

Did you know that the challenge for some types of college-level material is not to try to read faster, but to try to read slower?

"The cat sat on the mat," is not a complex thought, and it can be understood immediately.

Contrast that with,

Tomorrow, and tomorrow, and tomorrow,

Creeps in this petty pace from day to day,

To the last syllable of recorded time;

And all our yesterdays have lighted fools

The way to dusty death. Out, out, brief candle!

Life's but a walking shadow, a poor player,

That struts and frets his hour upon the stage,

And then is heard no more. It is a tale

Told by an idiot, full of sound and fury,

Signifying nothing.

That's Shakespeare, right?

Hamlet?
MacBeth?
The Tempest?

You can't read that fast, or if you do, you will skate right over the deeper meanings. Philosophy texts routinely require 10 minutes per page to parse the meaning. Students who are used to reading light novels at 60+ pages per hour may attempt a philosophy text at that rate and get to the end no wiser than when they started.

But if you try to read everything at just a few pages per hour, you will never finish all that you must read. So some things need to be skimmed. And skimming itself can be more effective if you know how to use the table of contents.

When you are reading non-fiction, the goal is always to challenge the text. Each sentence gets assessed – why is the author asserting this, what evidence is there that it might be so, what competing interpretations ought to be considered. Spend your time with an author engaged in battle like that and you will elevate your mind quite a bit, and deepen your understanding of the topic.

But don't read fiction that way! The goal with fiction is just the opposite. The author is going to create for you an experience, and your job is to immerse yourself in that experience, to willingly suspend your disbelief and completely live for a time in the world the author has created – its sights, sounds, language, and customs.

Once you are done reading, then comes the time to evaluate that experience – what did it do, what does it mean, what truths are illuminated?

Both fiction and non-fiction require active reading. You are to engage with the text as fully as you can.

Do not skip past words that you do not recognize; look them up. In fact, if you are reading a text that requires you to look up many words, it may be best to first get the meanings of all the new words, then go back to the text and read it again with the definitions fresh in your mind. It is difficult to follow the thread of a complex thought if you are interrupting that thread repeatedly with vocabulary checks. Separate *learning the words* from *using the words* and you will increase your odds of properly understanding what the author means.

Look up every word I don't understand??? That would REALLY slow me down!

Care about the device you are using to read. Paper books are designed for this. For example, it is very easy to highlight text and write margin notes on paper, and it might be easy on tablets, with the right hardware and software. But when you read on a phone, it is more difficult to interact with the text. And on a phone you lose context – you can't always see the text that is coming or has just gone. That may put too much space between your mind and the ideas you are trying to comprehend. It is like seeing a whole new world, but only through a peep hole.

Care, too, about the environment in which you read. If the book is worth reading at all, then it is worth giving it your entire attention. If you are multi-tasking in any way – even just listening to music – then your brain is only partially engaged and you will discover less and absorb less.

Highlighting text is a great way to keep track of themes. And if you're not writing in the margins, then you are probably not engaging with the text actively enough.

Highlighted text and margin notes are not just a good way to engage with the text and to focus your attention and avoid drifting off. They also help you to re-examine ideas later after you have learned more, or on a second read through.

If the book is important, try summarizing each paragraph after you read it. This will ensure not only that you have not drifted off, but also that you are actively engaging with the material. Saundra McGuire's *Teach Yourself to Learn*[50] explains why approaches like this work.

You can never read a great book twice; it is always different the second time. In fact, if a book is not worth reading twice, it is probably not worth reading once. And any time you read a great book only once, you have consigned yourself to just one version of that book for the rest of your life.

Say what? If a book is not worth reading twice, it is probably not worth reading once???

Why does the book seem to change with each re-read? Because the experience of reading the book combines your mind with the author's mind. My experience of a book is different from yours because what the author is getting at resonates differently for me than for you. Or at least different parts of the book hit differently. But then next time I read it, I am slightly different person from who I was before, so now the book seems different even to me – some parts that seemed inconsequential before this time capture me.

So you must learn how to read. You must read actively. If nothing else, at least slow down. It's no good to go to college, buy the books, and then only look as if you are reading them without really comprehending the essence of it. You might fool yourself, but you will not likely fool your professor.

And if you do fool the professor into thinking you understand something that you do not, the loss will be yours, not the professor's. And the loss will not be just the undiscovered insights the remain hidden in the book after you leave. You also lose the practice revealing such insights in future books.

Leave no book unconquered.

Bad books

How do I know that my professors won't assign any books that have mistakes?

You should, of course, choose your professors carefully. But your professors will certainly assign books that make incorrect arguments. And the errors you encounter will be mistakes worth considering, worth understanding – mistakes of the type you are likely to encounter again. Descartes' famous Meditation – the one where he concludes "I think therefore I am" – contains one of the greatest errors in all of Philosophy. The goal is not to take Descartes' words as gospel, but to discover where he went wrong, and why, and so what?

Stupid books

But what if the book is stupid?

In a bookstore you may encounter published things that are foolish and not worth your time. But you can safely assume that the texts assigned in college are worthy opponents, and you should confidently strive to interrogate their contents.

Looking up words

You're not serious about looking up every word I don't understand, are you?

Very serious indeed. If you don't know what a word means, then you can't fully understand the sentence. There's no use pretending that you read something and understood it. You're only fooling yourself.

Skimming versus reading

Maybe I can get the gist of the sentence without looking up every word, though?

The gist might be enough if you're just skimming, but it won't be enough when a close reading is required. In any case, get in the habit of looking up words. It's not a shame to not know a word; the shame is in not caring enough to look it up. Get used to demanding of yourself a deep understanding of the ideas you consider.

Book? What's a book?

Why are we even talking about books? I read everything online.

That's okay – everything we have discussed in this chapter applies to all kinds of text, whether they are available in printed books, e-books, PDFs, or just reading online.

Speed reading

I was always the fastest reader in my grade, and it become a competitive thing. I got a lot of praise for it. I actually studied speed-reading. It stopped working at college, because I would think I had read something but then couldn't answer the kinds of questions they were asking. The idea that you were allowed to read slower, actually encouraged to read slower, blew my mind. It went against everything I had been taught.

Chapter 17
Takeaways

- Some texts can only be read quite slowly, only a few pages per hour, or you won't understand them

- Don't skip words you don't know; look them up

- Read non-fiction by challenging the text

- Read fiction by allowing yourself to be entirely immersed in the experience

- Highlight the text and write notes in the margins to assist with your active reading and to help gather your thoughts

Chapter 18

How to Write

There is nobody whose writing cannot be improved, who could not benefit greatly from a good copy editor, including us, and including you.

Skilled writers soar on currents of language and meaning, while beginning writers hug the ground, haphazardly connecting nouns and verbs.

You can fly. Just a few things can make a huge difference.

Write! The first and most important is to write. Write and write and write. Write until the thoughts in your mind flow easily into text.

Read What You Write. You will never, ever turn in a draft that you have not first re-read yourself. Re-read everything you write, and make corrections. Read it out loud, and you will get a better sense of how it sounds to your readers. Almost nothing comes out just right the first time. Maybe you send text messages to friends without first re-reading them, but do not do that with emails to professors, and certainly not with class assignments.

Proof-read every email? I think not.

Get Feedback. Get feedback on your writing and take the feedback seriously. This is difficult for most students. Most people's intuition is to defend their writing choices or to feel miserable from the critique, neither of which makes you a better writer. The better practice is to try to understand why your reader suggests a different approach.

Step Back. Put some distance between you and your draft. One of the things that makes it difficult to assess your own writing is that your mind knows exactly what you are trying to express, so when you read your own writing, your mind resolves all the ambiguities correctly. Not so for your poor reader. But if you wait an hour, or a day, or a week, your ideas are not so fresh in your mind, and it is easier to perceive as your reader will perceive.

Read. As you master punctuation, grammar, and syntax, you will increasingly focus on semantics and style, which are advanced methods of conveying meaning with ever increasing precision and subtlety. Read and read and read. That will expose you to many authors whose different styles prove to be particularly effective for different purposes.

You will learn not to choose just any old word for your sentence. Each word does something slightly different, and you need to care about those differences and make each word count. If you do not, then your readers will not understand you clearly; it will be like seeing your thoughts through blurry glasses, or hearing them muffled through a wall. Powerful writing is clear, and conveys exactly what you intend. Even if your intention is to be ambiguous, the ambiguity can be conveyed unambiguously.

Get help with your writing. No one is born a good writer. Most people leave high school with only basic skills that leave a lot of room for improvement.

Start with Strunk & White. Start with the classic, *The Elements of Style* by Strunk & White. It's a short, easy, inexpensive book that anyone can understand and put to immediate use. Many of your readers are familiar with Strunk & White. Therefore, if you make the kind of writing mistakes that are mentioned in that book, your readers will think you have not read Strunk & White, and they will likely conclude that you are not serious about your writing

Already read Strunk & White? Read it again. Strunk & White will carry you across many mountains – not only grammar, but also composition and style. There is nothing we can recommend that is as short, good, and cheap as *The Elements of Style*.

There is online support, too – sites like the Purdue Online Writing Lab (OWL)[51] offer video tutorials on different aspects of writing.

Your college will support you: head to the writing center to get guidance and feedback. Nearly every college has one. It's free. They'll have lots of resources to help you write better, and they can recommend what is currently the best available guidance, in addition to being able to give you specific feedback on your writing.

Aspire to be a great writer. It is one of the most powerful skills you can acquire. You will discover that writing is thinking, and becoming a better writer will make you a better thinker. Eventually you will acquire the wisdom of the adage, "I don't know what I think until I write it down."

In addition to improving your thinking, improving your writing is one of the best ways to improve your job prospects. Good writers are always in demand, in every type of business, in every industry. If you can translate ideas into clear language, you have a marketable skill – plus, you become a fast, cogent correspondent.

And beyond that, it is very satisfying to write well, even if you only write notes to your family, comments on social media, and the occasional letter to the editor.

Re-Reading Everything

Proofreading everything, even emails, feels like a huge waste of time. I don't think I am going to do it. Often I only change a word or two anyway.

Proofreading is when you confirm that you wrote what you intended – no typographical or autocorrect errors. Editing is when you read for sense – does it express your meaning as well as possible? When you re-read, you are both proofreading and editing.

And the reason to do it is exactly as you said – you almost always make changes, even if it's only a word or two. And if you read it again you'll likely find even more ways to improve. That's how your writing improves: by re-writing.

There's something else, too. When you write anything – especially an email — you are asking someone else to take the time to read what you have written. The way you respect your readers' time is by being careful not to speak inefficiently – by writing as clearly and as concisely as possible.

Think of it this way: If it's not worth your time to read what you have written, why should it be worth anyone else's time?

Voice-to-text dictation

Are you kidding? Writing is as easy as talking. I just speak into the computer, and it creates text.

Be careful. Writing and speaking are very different. They have different purposes, and require different linguistic structures. Writing organizes your thoughts, and uses language to make up for the lack of verbal cues. Talking is for quickly, roughly conveying ideas with emotional affect. What works fine for oral communication will, if simply reduced to text, be undisciplined writing – inadequately structured, ambiguous, and difficult to comprehend. You may already be an effective speaker, but writing is a different skill, and one you must master. Voice-to-text may quickly get some words onto the page faster than your fingers can, but that is just the start, not the end, of your writing.

Writing Center

I like the idea of writing, until I get a blank screen in front of me, and then everything I thought I was going to say just vanishes. Then I write an okay first sentence, thinking that once I get started the words will come. But they don't come.

I went to my college's writing center, and they were super nice, and gave me a lot of helpful tips, but also some not useful tips. My college's writing center hires student tutors, and I think just like everything else, including professors, the people can be hit and miss. You have to pay attention to who you get.

I'm still not a great writer, but much better.

Re-writing

I always wanted to be a writer. I knew I could write. I planned to major in Creative Writing. I thought I didn't need any help from anyone, just practice. Totally wrong. Now I know that my 10th draft won't be as good as my 11th. That was the key to learning how to write for me. Not learning how to get started, but learning that it's never done.

Chapter 18
Takeaways

- To become a good writer, practice writing. Write and write until the thoughts in your mind flow easily into text

- Re-read and re-write. Never turn in a draft that you have not first re-read yourself

- Get feedback on your writing and take the feedback seriously

- Do not only overly rely on voice-to-text software. Writing is different from speaking

- Get help, from books on writing like Strunk & White, and from all the resources at your college's Writing Center

Chapter 19

How to Think

A primary purpose of college is to improve your thinking. We can't accomplish that in a chapter. But we can at least outline what we mean, so you have a target to aim at.

When we talk about clear, high-quality thinking, we mean several things.

Empirical Inquiry. Empirical thinking asks about facts in the world – how deep is the ocean, where is Kalamazoo, why does bread rise, was Abraham Lincoln really the 16th President? Empirical methods can tell us.

When you study natural sciences you are usually focusing on empirical thinking. The scientific method is a way of understanding empirical knowledge. The answers may be easy or difficult to uncover, but with the right equipment or methodology, most factual questions can be resolved with a high level of certainty.

Formal Logic. Next, there is logical thinking in the formal sense. Can you reason logically from empirically true premises to draw conclusions that are valid? Formal logic is quite mathematical, so it is possible to bring great precision to the question of whether, assuming your empirical premises are true, a specific conclusion follows logically or not.

Your Philosophy department offers a class in formal logic. If that class is not required, you should take it anyway. To leave college unfamiliar with the basic methods of logic would be an unforced error.

Informal Logic. Next, there is informal logic, frequently referred to as "Critical Thinking." Done correctly, critical thinking classes are interesting and engaging, because you can assess real-world examples. The usefulness of the curriculum is immediately apparent. And it is fun to see mistakes by public figures and in public forums – mistakes so simple that they can be refuted by a first-year college student. That's empowering, and tells you that you might have what it takes to be civically influential. Certainly critical thinking is a key skill for social engagement.

That seems disrespectful of public figures...

If you have a decent mastery of formal and informal logic, it will give you the confidence to join public discussions. That is you beginning to find your voice. And once you do join, because you have these skills, the quality of the public discussion will be improved. That will make everyone else happy, and it will make the world a better place, too.

Defense Against Propaganda. Ideally your critical thinking class will include a robust section explaining how propaganda works and demonstrating methods of dealing with it.

Optical illusions exploit defects in our visual processing system, forcing us to see things that do not exist, or preventing us from seeing things that are right in front of our noses.

Our cognitive processing systems have similar defects, and they are equally exploitable, which means that manipulative people can cause us to believe things that are not true, and disbelieve things that are true, and even to embrace an overall reality that is entirely false.

The Information Age potentially provides us with a wealth of knowledge. But it also exposes us to dangerous disinformation.

Knowing how an optical illusion works does not stop the illusion. Same with propaganda: knowing that you are being propagandized does not defeat the effect. So it is important to understand how propaganda works, and to always be vigilant when you encounter propaganda techniques.

If you're not getting a full dose of this in your critical thinking class, check with the library. The librarians sometimes offer instruction on media literacy and propaganda.

Problem Solving. Problem solving is the science of resolving practical challenges. I may need to get from here to there with no obvious means of doing it. There may be confounding factors, too, like I am broke, and stressed, and there is a deadline, and the consequences of failure are significant.

Problem solving involves surveying options, spotting issues, inventorying risks, identifying potential solutions, evaluating those solutions, and eventually choosing one. Good problem solvers don't just choose the most obvious solution, or the easiest or the cheapest; they find the best solution.

And if part of the problem is that the range of available solutions is inadequate, they do not accept a poor solution, but instead find a way to expand the range of options. And if they are good risk managers, then their proposed solutions come with backup plans, too.

Those who complain about frustrations at work are frequently victims of someone's poor problem-solving skills. People are constantly solving problems – maybe an idea needs to be communicated or a practice needs to be adjusted – but they often reach for the easiest and most obvious solutions, without seriously considering potential unintended consequences. As a result, their chosen solution may leave the organization no better off, and sometimes worse off. The fact that we are all solving problems all day does not mean that we should approach the task without discipline – just the opposite.

Creative Thinking. Creative thinking comes into play when the obvious or traditional solutions are inadequate. Some people are naturally good at "thinking outside the box," and others freeze when challenged to approach something in an unfamiliar way.

But everyone can be better at it.

Creative thinking isn't only useful for solving practical problems, either. Creativity can help us express ideas and emotions in compelling ways, and perhaps challenge or expand our perspectives – we call this art.

Exercising creativity can be both satisfying and rewarding. In your own life you will often encounter old habits that die hard, even though the habits have stopped serving their original purpose (if they ever did).

But moving beyond what you have always done requires not just courage and adjustment, but also the ability to imagine the world different from how it is. Sometimes that's easy, like imagining a world where private cars don't pollute. But sometimes the imaginative challenge is more difficult, like imagining a world where there don't need to be private cars, or perhaps not even roads.

Some challenges just need problem solving skills, whereas others require a good dose of creative thinking.

Interpretation. We all have experiences that we need to make sense of. Our ability to make sense of them determines how well our mental map of the universe and of ourselves improves, or whether instead we take away from events all the wrong lessons.

Literary, artistic, and historical interpretation are where this skill gets practiced most.

Have you ever read an unhelpful movie review? Did it tell you too much, or too little, or was it focused on the wrong things? Or have you ever read a movie review that helped you better understand a move that you had already seen?

Making sense of a work of art, theatrical production, or historical event – or some of the drama in our own lives – requires nuanced and layered thinking. We must simultaneously attend to important detail while not losing track of the larger themes, detecting the harmony and conflict that may make a particular interpretation more or less compelling.

In high school, History students memorize facts, and English students are taught to identify irony, paradox, metaphor, and ambiguity. They are discovering the building blocks of meaning.

But this is only the beginning of interpretation, not the end. Do not confuse a pile of bricks with an actual building.

Why did the post-civil war United States abandon Reconstruction? What are we to take away from Shakespeare's *MacBeth*?

These questions require interpretive thinking. There isn't a single, simple, sure answer, as we find with empirical questions. But interpretive questions are just as important as the boiling point of water, so we need to master this kind of thinking, too.

Natural sciences explain physical phenomena, like why water boils, but literature explains emotional and psychological and social phenomena. So do sociology, psychology, and anthropology. Connecting those dots allows you to understand how the world works, and how your workplace works, and how your family and community work, and they help you find your place.

Those Humanities classes don't look like they're training you on the nature of emotional, psychological, and social phenomena any more than running tires looks like playing football.

But the Humanities are just as surely training you for the playing field — the playing field of your own life.

It's no wonder that high school students become bored and disillusioned with learning, if they feel like they are confronting a pile of bricks with no chance to build anything.

In college, there is a better a chance to practice interpretive thinking, and it will allow you to unlock truths that cannot be discovered any other way. Make sure you take classes that help you hone your interpretive skills.

Moral Thinking. Finally we come to moral thinking, the most troublesome of the thought types we will be covering.

Factual or "empirical" questions are questions about how the world is.

Moral thinking is not about how the world is, but how it ought to be. Moral thinking typically starts with the word "ought" or "should," like, "There ought to be a law," or "You should change your ways."

But careful, these words can also be used in a non-moral sense, like, "You ought to use nails instead of screws if you want that structure to survive an earthquake."

Here we are using "ought" in the prudential sense, which is problem-solving: if you want a specific outcome, there is a better way to achieve it. But we are not necessarily recommending the outcome. There might be good reasons not to make a structure earthquake proof. Perhaps the structure is located in a place that does not get earthquakes, or the structure is a bird house.

We are also not using "ought" in the moral sense when we tell ourselves what to do, like "I really ought to get a haircut." Possibly true, but it is my own business.

We use ought in the moral sense when we are directing that a particular action be taken, because it will make things better, and the action impacts more than just me.

Moral questions typically involve conflicting priorities, and people often feel strongly. Some people want a road here; others want to preserve the tree. Now we have a moral question. How do we resolve it?

I'm still for the tree!

Not only are the right answers to moral questions often difficult to discern, we may disagree whether something even is a moral question.

Whether I should go bike-riding this afternoon is probably not a moral question if it does not impact other people. But if I choose to go bike riding instead of celebrating my partner's birthday, then my decision might take on moral dimensions. But what if my partner doesn't care very much, or cares way too much, or thinks they don't care but decides later that they did? How does that get weighed?

Bike riding is a moral question?

It is important to determine whether a question has a moral dimension because the principles governing the correct resolution of moral issues are different from those used for other types of thinking.

We normally resolve moral issues with the help of "rules of thumb," like *Be polite to the people around you*, *Don't break the law*, and *Don't lie*. Rules like that will normally keep us away from moral hazards without our having to do a lot of moral analysis.

You may have been incorrectly taught that such rules of thumb are themselves the underlying moral principles that we must follow.

But the rules of thumb are not the final word. There are unusual circumstances in which being polite, obeying the law, and telling the truth would actually not be the morally right thing to do.

How could obeying the law be morally wrong?

You don't believe it? Suppose a law says that no vehicles may be driven in the park, but someone is seriously hurt and an ambulance needs to get through. Is it morally permissible to drive the ambulance in the park after all? Indeed, it may be morally required that we break this law under these circumstances.

Similarly, I may have decided to run a stop light on my bicycle. I have surely done something illegal. But is it immoral? If it endangers or vexes other travelers at the intersection, then I have entered the realm of moral jeopardy. But if I can be certain that there is nobody anywhere near or even in sight of the intersection, then the decision may not impact anyone but me.

A proper assessment of moral thinking would require a book-length treatment.

If you read such a book, you will discover that not everyone's opinion about right or wrong is equally valid, and we cannot escape moral dilemmas by saying that everyone has a right to their own opinion. This way lies moral relativism, and it is not correct.

Instead, most moral philosophers, like most religions, have concluded that the general answer to moral questions is not that might makes right, or that I should get whatever I want. Instead, it runs closer to the Golden Rule: Do unto others as you would have others do unto you. This principle requires equal consideration of everyone's interests, yours and mine and anybody else impacted by the decision.

That's a lot of work! You must be over-thinking it!

Properly decoding that maxim, putting it on a sound logical foundation, and then applying it in real world situations involving our families, our friends, our communities, and our nations, is the work of moral thinking.

Critical thinking in public

Don't you think it's disrespectful to challenge public figures or to expose errors in their thinking?

On the contrary, it is the highest form of respect to take someone's argument seriously and to analyze it conscientiously. After all, we're all after the same prize: the truth.

However, what might be disrespectful is if a famous person or a public official makes an argument that is false and easy to debunk. Either they did not take the time to check their own thinking before recommending it to others, or they don't care whether they make work for others to sort out their flawed thinking. That's disrespectful of us.

Religion and Morality

I thought religion and morality were the same thing, and only religions could answer moral questions.

One reason we study Philosophy is to disabuse ourselves of such notions. Religions offer many different answers, but they tend to be based on faith. Philosophers attempt a firmer foundation for their answers.

Calculating truth

We had to take formal logic at my college. Formal logic was a trap; it started out so easy that I was bored, and then suddenly it was algebra; but instead of calculating numbers you are calculating truth. Who even knew that was possible?

Being critical is not criticizing

I thought critical thinking would be easy, because I already know how to be critical, and I argue a lot. Then it turned out that critical thinking isn't about criticizing, but about a whole methodology about measuring truth, based on evaluating evidence and challenging assumptions, which I had no idea about, and was totally different from what I thought. I never argue the way I used to, after taking informal logic. I'm also not as certain about things as I used to be. There are more reasons for things than I may know. But when I do have an opinion, at least I'm confident about why I have it.

Chapter 19

Takeaways

- You must master many different kinds of thinking: Empirical inquiry, Formal logic, Critical Thinking, Defense against Propaganda, Interpretive Thinking, Problem Solving, Creative Thinking, and Moral Thinking

- Clear, disciplined thinking is the single most valuable skill you can develop, especially if you have also mastered a broad range of thinking skills

Chapter 20

How to Learn

If you think you already know how to read and how to write, you surely already know how to learn. But as with reading and writing, you will need to improve your game to fully take advantage of what college has to offer.

Much of primary and secondary education is involved with memorization of things like times tables and the Krebs Cycle and who was the 16th President. Certainly there are things worth memorizing, and you will do some memorizing in college. But higher education is mostly not about that.

Another kind of learning that you also need to master is to understand the material you are confronting. Just as it is very easy to glaze over and drift off when reading a book, it is very easy to hear words and ideas without really processing them.

One good way to test whether you are following the ideas is to try to explain them to someone else. If your friends and roommates get tired of listening to you, you can talk to a wall or to a pet. The point is to reformulate the material in your own words in the form of a complete explanation – what and why. If you can't do that, then you haven't learned it yet.

But the most important learning goal in higher education is not the mere cognition of information – as important as that may be[52] – but the journey into the unknown.

In college you will encounter ideas, contexts, and ways of thinking that are entirely new. And the ability to engage effectively with unfamiliar concepts is the learning ability to be acquired.

Imagine you walk into a room and nothing is as you expect it to be. You do not recognize any of the people. In fact, they are Martians. The furniture, lighting, and music are not like anything you have seen before. Even the shape of the room is unconventional. Their language is strange. And most of all, you have no idea what they are doing or why.

There are many poor ways to respond. You could tell the Martians that their way of being is improper. You could politely set to arranging things into a more earth-like aesthetic. Or you might just panic and flee.

What learning to learn requires is curiosity, patience, and a willingness to understand. That understanding does not come from measuring things against your preconceived notions, but by trying to understand things on their own terms.

There is a world of difference between judging the Martians based on Earth standards, and understanding the world as the Martians do.

Instead of focusing on the strangeness of their green skin and antennae, you might realize how suffocating is our thick atmosphere, how burdensome our gravity, and what a great distance Earthlings keep from each other, even when they stand close together.

What if the Martians are here to attack?

These insights drawn from the Martians' experience make visible our implicit assumptions, the ones that we take for granted, and which are invisible to us until illuminated by considering an unfamiliar viewpoint.

Although you will likely not encounter any actual Martians during your college years, there is a good chance that you will encounter Physicists, Philosophers, Art Historians, Anthropologists, Sociologists, Mathematicians, Chemists, and Linguists whose language and perspectives are nearly as strange.

Nurture your curiosity by trying to understand the unfamiliar people and new ways of thinking that surround you in college.

You might have great reasons for being interested in a particular major before you arrive, but if you are curious and ready to learn, then you will consider the possibility that there is another major that you did not know about that might be an even better fit. You should not be too eager to burrow into your specialty without having explored the diversity around you.

This matters immensely to your education because in your life, and in your career, and even in your interactions with extended family, you will encounter strange new worlds with unfamiliar cultural norms and unexpected ways of thinking. Your ability to make sense of and respond effectively to new situations will sometimes determine whether you fail or succeed in your future endeavors, both personal and professional.

This approach to learning requires active engagement. You don't just assume that Martians are good or bad, and you don't just wait for your professor to tell you the right answer and take their word for it. Instead, you must engage your curiosity to deeply understand for yourself.

That means that learning isn't something that happens to you; it's something that you make happen. It's not like joining a club and waiting for something to happen; it's like joining a club to make something happen.

So engage your curiosity to deeply understand the various Martians you will encounter. You are of course free to reject them. But until you understand them as thoroughly as they understand themselves, you risk that your judgment will be based on an incomplete or inaccurate understanding.

Good learners set aside their preconceived notions and time-tested biases, and instead try to understand a discipline and its methodology on its own terms. What are historical truths, and literary truths, and how do they differ from philosophical truths, and mathematical truths? How can they be useful in your life?

I kind of like my biases, though. They seem mostly right.

You may dislike poetry because you have had some bad experiences with it. You might have been required to memorize poems that were insipid, or that had forced rhymes, or that were incomprehensible. Your job now is to set aside your negative bias and to discover why poetry even exists. And poetry does not merely exist; it is considered so important that each year the United States honors a Poet Laureate, an official poet of the nation, who serves a two-year term. Find out why.

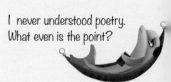

I never understood poetry. What even is the point?

Most things exist for a good reason. So when you find something disagreeable, like opera, bureaucracy, or quantum mechanics, the challenge is to discover what they are made for, and to consider them in their best light. After you have deeply understood them, you don't have to like them. All of your original critiques may turn out to be valid. But now they will be well-informed critiques, and not superficial prejudices. That increases the reliability of your critiques, even if your views have not changed much substantively.

But more often that not your views will change. That's the nature of understanding things more deeply, and the reason why learning to learn is so important.

Even if you do not move to Mars, you may decide that you enjoy the Martians' company and that you benefit from their perspectives.

Following your passion

When you talk about engaging with unfamiliar ideas, are you saying I should take classes that I am not interested in, like Literature, Sociology, Chemistry, and Politics? I thought we were supposed to be following our passions?

It's not either/or; it's both. Your major is where you follow your passion. But add to that as much breadth as possible so you can learn other ways of thinking. Those other ways of thinking will specifically help you solve thorny problems in your future.

The practical value of breadth

How will learning other ways of thinking help me with thorny problems?

You will need, in life and in work, to interact effectively with those who think differently. Sometimes you will need to oppose something and argue against it effectively. But you can't fight something that you do not understand.

If you leave college not knowing how chemists, journalists, and anthropologists imagine worlds, and the nature of different viewpoints, some enterprises and relationships may be more difficult, and some important skills may be underdeveloped, like relationship building, social awareness, and managing conflict.

Dangers of curiosity

I'm not sure your approach to learning is wise. Anything could be a threat. What if the Martians turn out to be hostile – then our attempts to understand them could be dangerous, like in the movies.

Close. We absolutely want to be attuned to potential threats when confronting the unknown. But at the same time, we do not want to be inventing threats that aren't there and then reacting to our imagination.

The important part is that we don't have to choose. We can be as open-minded and curious and interested as learning requires, and simultaneously watch for evidence of danger. The possibility of danger does not justify closing our minds to the possibility of something much better.

The risks and benefits of biases

Are you really telling us to give up our biases? Biases are like snap decisions, and they often reflect wisdom and tell us how our heart feels. I dislike opera, without knowing much about it, and I don't feel like I need to know much more about it. What's wrong with that?

That's right; some assumptions are based on evidence – even if it is limited evidence – and prove to be correct.

Making decisions with incomplete information is an important skill, and something we do every day, because we rarely have complete information about anything. So that kind of bias is just a fact of life.

However, just as some of our biases and assumptions that are based on inadequate information will nonetheless prove to be correct, others will prove to be wrong.

The challenge with college-level learning is first to become aware of our biases – beliefs that are based on only partial information – and then be willing to challenge those beliefs and to gather additional evidence, getting closer to the truth. Sometimes the truth will be as we suspected, and other times we might be surprised – but only if we keep an open mind to the possibility of surprise.

Unfamiliar ways of thinking

I started in the social sciences and took a class in the Humanities (literature) and I was loving it, until I got my first paper back with a really bad grade, and realized there was a huge disconnect between what I thought was going on and what was actually going on. They were looking for a totally different approach to thinking than I was used to. The TA for the course was really nice, though, and explained how to think in the Humanities. Eventually I figured it out. Not right away, but in time to switch my major to Literature.

Chapter 20

Takeaways

- Learning is not mostly about memorizing things. And it is not just about understanding things. It is also about opening your mind to alternatives

- Biases and prejudices are not necessarily bad; a stereotype can be accurate. They are only dangerous if we are unwilling or unable to challenge them and revise our thinking based on new facts or better analysis

Chapter 21

How to Disagree

And finally, college level work requires that you be skilled at disagreeing.

An unskillful disagreer might attack their opponent with insults, indignation, and accusations.

That all might be warranted, but it is still not the right way to go about it.

That I can do!

Instead, we must start with the principle identified in the prior chapter, which is that we are to try to understand the competing view as best we can, on its own terms. Perhaps in the end it will prove foolish. But, nonetheless, what good can be said for it? What is its purpose?

You can't disagree with a position that you do not actually understand. Then you are not disagreeing, you are merely bloviating. Bloviating can be immensely satisfying while you're doing it, but it offers no lasting benefit, and may harm your standing with others.

So to disagree with someone, you need to first understand them, which will require some respectful inquiries about their key points.

They like horror films, and you do not.

Don't tell them they have monstrously; bad taste in movies. Instead, try to understand why they like horror films, what about it is pleasant or meaningful. Or if they find horror films disconcerting, why do they like that feeling?

Once you have learned enough to understand the nature of your disagreement, you can now practice expressing it respectfully. *"I now understand your personal attraction to horror films [listing those reasons], but have you considered the possible negative effect they have on others, either by propagating fear, anxiety, and dread, or by normalizing anti-social behavior?"* There might even be some research on this point.

This is not just a more civilized way to interact, compared to lobbing invectives and insults. It is also more effective.

By demonstrating that you have understood the person's argument, and by showing with your politeness that you care about their feelings even if you disagree with their thoughts, you create for them the emotional space to consider your competing argument. In other words, by opening yourself to the possibility that you may be wrong, you also open your colleague to the possibility that you may be right.

And that kind of civil discourse not only helps you to prevail in this argument. It also helps you in future arguments, because observers will assign more respect to you as a thinker, and be more willing to engage with your ideas, if they know that you will take them seriously and treat their ideas with respect.

Indeed, the entire enterprise of the Academy is awash in disputes involving matters far weightier than one's taste in movies. For that environment of healthy discourse to thrive, it needs to be done in ways that are productive and efficient, and which do not exhaust the participants.

Your job is not to agree with everything you read or hear, but to challenge ideas – both your own ideas and also ideas that you encounter. But challenge them thoughtfully, empathetically, and respectfully.

Keep in mind, too, that you may disagree with someone without knowing that you are doing it. It's really easy to disagree incorrectly if you don't even know you are disagreeing.

Every time you talk you might be saying something that someone else finds disagreeable. So don't wait until a disagreement becomes obvious to start respecting other people's positions. Instead, assume whenever you say something that one or more listeners may disagree, and be careful not to disrespect their potential contrary opinions before you have even heard them.

How do you respect something you don't know about yet? Easy. Just leave room, when you speak, for the possibility of competing views.

That means don't start from a position of strong certainty. If you claim to be certain of something before you have had the chance to hear competing views, chances are your statements will be off-putting and lack credibility.

Instead, start with something gentler, like "I think," or "It seems," or "It may be."

Even if you are certain, you don't have to express that certainty early in the discussion. There will be time for it later. And who knows – maybe someone will say something that makes you less certain, and you'll be glad you didn't start out on a limb.

But isn't that dishonest?

Showing vulnerability

You said to pretend in my discussions that I am less certain than I really am. Is that garden variety dishonesty, or are we setting a trap?

Neither. The goal isn't so much to pretend that you are uncertain, but to allow yourself to be uncertain.

For people who have made their mark by being right and by pressing their points, the challenge in college is to not be so sure of yourself. This is difficult for some people, and goes against both experience and intuition.

But the reality is that the technique of being the smartest one in the room, and pushing your way through, offers diminishing returns as you encounter more smart people, more different perspectives, and more difficult problems. And that's what college is going to give you.

Ideally, you will experience genuine uncertainty until you thoroughly understand the competing viewpoints, but if all you can muster is 1% uncertainty, then express the 1%.

When to disagree

My way of disagreeing is just to agree to disagree. I don't need everyone to agree with me. I'll just keep to my own views. Live and let live, you know?

We certainly should be tolerant of those with preferences different from ours. But it is important not to confuse misunderstandings, disagreements of facts, and disagreements of values. We should not accept misunderstandings and disagreements about facts. We can use our thinking and learning skills to avoid misunderstandings, and we can use our research skills to avoid disagreements about facts. We need to understand each other and to agree on facts.

Disagreements about values are a different matter. Aesthetic disagreements – you like one type of clothing and I like another – are indeed to be tolerated. But if the disagreements involve moral conflicts – for example, if others are facing significant risk or harm – then we must not walk away from the situation with a casual shrug.

Why to disagree

I used to just hate discussion groups because people were always disagreeing with each other, and honestly that made me uncomfortable. It was like everyone was arguing all the time, which reminded me of the worst moments of living at home. I had to first figure out that arguing can be good. Second, I had to realize that some of the students weren't actually arguing, they were just being obnoxious. Once I understood that, and could identify it, I could help steer the discussion toward good forms of confrontation, and away from bad ones. That helped everyone somewhat, but most of all it helped me.

Helping others to disagree

I was a graduate student TA. Leading discussion groups was the most important part of the job. But it was so hard! More than half the students really did not want to participate – usually because they were shy, or did not want to show ignorance in front of their peers. For the ones who spoke, I could pretty quickly figure out where they were stuck and help them. But for the ones who wouldn't speak, I couldn't do much. The students I treasured were the few brave ones who were always willing to share their thoughts, because not only did that let me help them, it also gave others courage to speak, so I could help even more students.

Chapter 21

Takeaways

- Disagreeing isn't being disagreeable; it is a tool for improving our understanding. You should not ignore or hide disagreements, but handle them respectfully

- You should start by attempting to fully understand the opposing viewpoint

- Disagreeing respectfully fosters more discussion, and improves others' willingness to consider your views

Chapter 22

How to Use AI at College

As with all tools, there is a right way and a wrong way to use AI Assistants like OpenAI's ChapGPT®, Microsoft's Copilot®, Google's Gemini®, Anthropic's Claude®, or any question-answering tool that relies on large language models.

Students have always been able to buy their way out of college thinking.

Expensive test-taking services and paper-writing services offered to do all of the work – literally taking the tests or writing the papers. This kind of assistance has always been forbidden, but never eradicated.

Less extreme forms of assistance, like study guides (for example, SparkNotes®, CliffNotes®, or even Wikipedia®) promise to tell students what is contained in difficult or lengthy works without the students' actually having to read or grapple with the text.

Most professors do not welcome the use of these secondary sources, and often actively discourage their use, because the grappling with text is the actual thinking exercise to be done, and that is what the secondary sources are reducing or eliminating.

Other minor forms of assistance are non-controversial, like calculators, spell-check, grammar helpers (like Grammarly®), which most professors do not mind, because they automate the tedious parts of the work so students can focus on the important parts.

And of course targeted assistance with basic skills, like the kind of one-on-one tutoring offered by a college's Learning Center, is actively encouraged.

So when an AI system offers to identify and fix writing errors, evaluate your paper and suggest improvements, or even to actually read your assigned texts and write your paper for you, that's not really new.

What's new is that these systems are simple, convenient, universally available, and inexpensive or even free.

Should you use them, or should it be against the rules to get this kind of assistance at college?

Colleges are still figuring out how to deal with this technology.

But we can tell you how it is likely to come out, and how you can use AI to improve your education and make you smarter, rather than taking away from your education by displacing the very important learning that is a primary purpose of attending college in the first place.

There are three basic steps to most of the college-level work that AIs are offering help with.

First comes **research**, which is the gathering of materials relevant to an issue.

Next comes **analysis**, which is making sense of the research materials you have gathered – do they actually say the things attributed to them? Are there conflicts or disagreements among the sources? What is the range of ideas? Are we missing anything?

Finally comes **synthesis and evaluation**, which is what happens when you solve a problem or write a paper making an argument. You are trying to make sense of the sources, drawing out potential implications and competing interpretations, weighing the evidence, and making suggestions.

Using AI for Research. Research is ripe for automating, and you should normally take all the help you can get.[53]

There is no reason for you to walk to the library, and wander through shelves, and then leaf through pages, trying to find exactly what you want if a search engine can simply hand you exactly what you want. Search engines like Google automate the footwork so you can get right to the thinking.

That could save me a lot of time, if I can just cite the AI!

Using AIs for research is just like that – they can find relevant sources, facts and search terms – and it can be very fast and helpful – even though you still have to read and interpret the material.

Using AI for Analysis. Using the AI for analysis is a much riskier proposition, but it's not very different from using any secondary source that happens to be right on point.

When you are memorizing facts, the goal is just to identify the key facts and memorize them. So if that's the task, then you want to find the best summary available and memorize it.

But more often in college the challenge is to think it through yourself. There are some things worth memorizing, but college mostly doesn't want to store information in your head. Computers do data storage better. Instead, colleges are trying to teach you to make sense of a lot of data – to analyze and interpret.

So professors tend to dislike when, instead of trying to grapple with difficult ideas, you just go find someone else's analysis and adopt it as your own. It could be a great analysis, better than you might have done yourself. But the professor doesn't want you to find the best analysis; they could do that themselves. They want you to practice analyzing.

So when you can't make sense of some difficult material and you ask the AI what it means, you are probably short-circuiting the learning process and short-changing your education – if the learning task was to analyze the material.

Using AI for Synthesis and Evaluation. The higher levels of mental work are to synthesize a number of different sources, creating something new, building arguments based on competing and conflicting views, and assessing the results. That's usually what happens when you are writing a paper or completing a project.

There might even be nothing wrong with using AIs to help with gathering the analyses, if the primary educational goal were to synthesize those sources and develop and express strong arguments.

But using the AI for synthesis is almost always a bad idea.

What we want the AI for is to set the stage so that we can practice some serious thinking. If the AI actually does the most difficult and most serious thinking, then it is getting the college education, not us.

Imagine you are a painter. You don't want to go out in the forest and forage for dyes, and manufacture paint, and gather hairs that could be bound into brushes. You want to automate that work, so you can get to the creative part, which is the actual painting.

We might welcome a robot that handed us all the tools we needed to paint. But once the robot picks up the brush and starts painting for us, because it can do a better job than we can, and faster, then the robot's assistance is actually a problem.

So, too, with AI's helping with the thinking tasks in college.

Even though too much help with the thinking tasks of college has always been available, there are two reasons why the situation is much worse now with AIs than before.

First, there used to be significant barriers to getting too much help. Paper-writing services, for example, were expensive, and disreputable. And the people who might do your work for you, like friends or tutors, might themselves be inclined to limit just how much help they would give.

Even if you wanted to over-rely on secondary sources, it wasn't always easy to find a secondary source right on point, if there even was one. And at the very least you'd have to read and understand the secondary source to decide if it was useful.

But AIs can summarize any topic at any degree of detail and they will not hesitate to give you as much help as you want, no questions asked, fast and free.

So it is really easy to get too much help. Too easy.

Second, it's very difficult to know when you are getting too much help.

How can I get too much help? When I'm working at a job, I'll want all the help I can get!

You might start in a safe place, like asking for help with your research or guidance about how to make your writing better.

But gradually, almost imperceptibly, students who start out relying on the AI for time-savings and helpful advice may find themselves asking the AI not only to check their spelling and grammar, but to improve and expand the analysis, to strengthen the writing, and to enrich the analysis, synthesis, and evaluation in ways that the student could not do themselves.

Worse, the students may not even take the time to learn from the AI's example so that they could at least get some benefit.

The lack of guardrails is a real problem. A student could ask an AI to improve their work in 20 ways and the AI will likely do so. That's no different from asking a tutor to identify ways that a work could be improved.

But whereas a tutor should explain what they are doing and why, there is nothing that forces the student to closely examine all the changes made by an AI. Nor will the AI likely explain why it made those changes and not other changes, or why the changes it made represent improvements and not degradations.

It is on the students to do that work, and often they will not do it. Or even if they try, they might not do it well. And students typically have no way of knowing whether they are doing it well.

So colleges hope that AI could be really helpful in providing students with guidance. But colleges also fear that students might misuse this technology, either intentionally or inadvertently, so that the AI is doing most of the thinking and learning, and the student is partially or mostly removed from the education process.

Your job is to use AI to make it easier for you to think and learn, without letting the AI do the thinking or learning.

It's like letting a robot drive you to the gym, but not letting the robot actually lift any of the weight for you.

Can you use an AI to optimize the settings on the aerobics machine, but you still do all the aerobic work? It seems like you might.

Can you let a driving AI monitor your speed, run the windshield wipers, and manage the bright headlights, but you still maintain control – you decide where to go, and even how fast? Seems easy.

Then the driving AI offers to maintain the distance between the next car and keep you in your lane. Then it tells you the best time to change lanes. Then it recommends an alternate route. Soon it starts telling you about potential stops along the way that you didn't even know about.

You might end up with a better, safer trip. But at some point you will no longer be the one driving.

Your challenge with using AI in college is to make sure that you are always the driver.

Getting help from AIs

Don't you agree that using AI won't hurt me in my job because AIs will be common in the workplace. Knowing how to use them will help me in my job – in fact, it will be a job requirement!

AIs do some kinds of work better than humans, just as calculators are faster and more reliable than humans at calculating. That means there are no longer jobs for humans to calculate numbers, but humans can nonetheless incorporate calculators into jobs that require higher-level skills.

So, too, with AI. Many basic information processing jobs will go away. Spell-checking has already mostly been automated, and much more will follow.

The point is that the reason you are writing the paper is to develop the thinking skills required to write the paper. The thing you are thinking about isn't as important.

For example, if your professor has asked you to consider in Mary Shelley's Frankenstein whether there are important similarities between the monster and its creator, that's not because you will need in your life or your career to return to this particular question, but because spotting similarities is a skill that you should develop and that you will be able to use in a thousand ways that have nothing to do with Frankenstein.

But if the AI writes the paper for you, you get a good argument and no thinking skills. That's exactly the opposite of what you want. The particular argument doesn't matter and the thinking skills do.

Citing AI Research

So if I let the AI do the research for me, how do I cite the AI for whatever it gives me?

Citing an AI is like citing your Uncle Bob. Your uncle and the AI may be smart, and may be right, but they are not academically citable sources. They are also not verifiable sources. The next person who asks the AI or your Uncle Bob may get a different answer.

Instead of citing the AI, read the materials that the AI has found for you, and confirm that they say what you think they do, and then cite those sources.

That's how you would handle what you learned from a Google search, and it's the right way to use AI, too.

AIs on the job

But all workplaces will be using AIs, so I should practice now, right?

Nobody will pay you to ask the AI a question. They can ask the AI themselves. So any time you are using an AI, you are specifically not developing skills that will be economically valuable.

It's okay to use AI for research and to get to the higher-level tasks, the way engineers use calculators. But if you end up relying on the AI to do your thinking for you, you are not building future job skills, but instead preparing to do work that will be replaced by an AI.

The job you want to prepare for is not asking the AI questions, but evaluating the AI's responses. That requires the thinking skills we discussed in Chapter 19. You develop those skills by writing the paper yourself.

Chapter 22
Takeaways

- Using AI to automate the research process is usually a good thing

- Using AI to help you understand difficult or complex material is a bad idea if part of the assignment's purpose was to practice making sense of difficult or complex material

- Using AI to write your paper, solve your problem, or do your thinking is a bad idea, even if you could get away with it, because then you will leave college with underdeveloped thinking skills, which was one of the most important reasons you were spending your time and money on the education

Chapter 23

New Expectations

We said in Chapter 4 that if you approach college as if it were 13th grade, you are going to commit a lot of unforced errors. The sum of all those errors can be very costly. So you need to understand the new and different expectations that you are facing as a college student.

We are going to look at the amount of work that is expected, the quality of work that is expected, and the kinds of interactions with the faculty, grad students, and administration that are expected.

You can always decide you don't want to do what is expected. But in order to make an informed decision, you need to know what those expectations are.

Do I have to go to office hours? Do I have to speak in discussion groups? Can I take extra classes? Do I have to buy the course text? Can I audit a class? Can the prerequisite be waived? Can I slip into class late? Can I miss class if my job requires it? Can I work more than half-time? Should I try to live on campus? Can I text the professor a simple question? Let's find out.

How much work to expect – quantity

The amount of work required in college is a simple equation. For every in-class hour, you are expected to work at least two hours outside of class, reading, writing, and preparing.

So if an average full-time course load includes about 15 hours of in-class time, then you will be spending at least an additional 30 hours outside class, which adds up to at least 45 hours. At least.

You can expect new readings every class: essays, stories, chapters, novellas, or book excerpts, times multiple classes. It will take a long time if you read all that in a way that allows you to understand the materials deeply by challenging a non-fiction text or fully immersing yourself in fiction. And that is in addition to attending classes, participating in discussions, and writing papers about those readings. And each of those papers will go through many drafts. And there is recommended reading, too.

In other words, **college is more than a full-time job.** And if you participate in extra-curricular activities – like student government, residential life, theater, sports, activities, clubs, socializing, and more – as you should – then college is way more than a full-time job, and you will not have time for much else.

How much work to expect – quality

You are expected to put in a serious effort. Your instructors will easily detect when you are blowing off an assignment. They can recognize a superficial effort not only because they can compare your results to that of your classmates, but also because they may have taught the class many times and can compare your effort to that of many other students.

Nothing puzzles professors more than when they tell a class that they need to put in more effort, and the students then do so, and the overall quality of the work improves. Why didn't the students just try hard originally? Why would you ever turn in something that wasn't your best effort?

The truth is that for education to work everyone must make a good faith effort. You should expect your instructors to try very hard – to carefully craft the curriculum, the discussions, and the assignments, and to review your work with a professional eye toward evaluating and supporting your learning.

But the opposite is also true: your instructors expect you to do your part. They expect you to take the class seriously and try hard. If you are having trouble, they expect you to ask for help, and not let yourself drown.

Class Attendance. You should attend class. You'd be surprised how many things you learn when you're not trying, and how much there is to learn about people and processes simply by watching yourself with others trying to learn something.

Of course there are more practical reasons to attend class; you don't know what you're going to be missing until you miss it, and then you still can't know what you missed because you missed it.

If you ask someone what happened in class, they'll likely say, "Not much." That's not because not much happened, but because short-term memory is such that their experience of the class is not recorded in their minds in a way that can be easily replayed. Indeed, even if you had a video recording of the class, which could be easily replayed, watching would be a pale version of actually being there -- which is one reason, incidentally, that online classes are so fraught. Online learning is super-convenient, and it has some undeniable advantages. But you don't always know what you are missing compared to the in-person experience.

Most of all, if someone has gone to all the trouble of building a college, and you have gone to all the trouble and expense of enrolling, it's most of the way to crazy to not attend the classes. It's like climbing up an apple tree at the perfect moment in autumn, then finding the ripest fruit, and instead of picking it and eating it, you just climb down again.

Sometimes you will not be able to attend class. You might be sick, or have a true emergency. Here is what to do: (1) Alert the instructor that you will be absent; (2) Arrange to get notes about what you will miss, typically from a classmate; (3) Attempt an alternate arrangement – sometimes work can be submitted early or late, for example. If you have a good excuse, say it.

If you do not have a good excuse, then you should go to class, but do not under any circumstances tell a lie that sounds like a good excuse. Not only are lies often discovered, but they hurt your integrity even if they are not discovered, because you start to think of yourself as someone who lies to solve their problems. This is very unhealthy for your psyche. Instead, practice integrity by admitting to the actual state of affairs, or if that is not possible, simply say, "I have a conflict and cannot attend." That excuse won't win you any awards, but at least it won't separately harm you.

Withdrawing. Sometimes life deals you lemons, and you will have to withdraw from a class entirely, or even from college entirely. The Registrar has rules and deadlines and consequences about how to do that. They are what they are. Learn them, and make your choices.

Just don't freak out. Sometimes the brave thing to do is to face your fears, don't withdraw, and

navigate the stormy parts of your life with a steady hand. But sometimes the brave thing to do is to recognize when you need to make a change, and be willing to re-chart your course temporarily or indefinitely.

The best answer will depend on your situation.

But the worst thing you can do is to hide from the problem, to disappear. Your college is absolutely ready to help you think through the problem – it happens to students constantly – but you have to resist the feelings of panic or shame or inadequacy or whatever makes you afraid to ask for help. Students face this kind of situation all the time. There is nothing wrong with you.

Get as much help as you can. Academic advisors and psychological counselors are available. Get their advice. And if you decide you need to leave, know the conditions under which you can return easily without having to re-apply for admission.

Reasonable course loads. The inverse of withdrawing from a class or from college is to go overload, taking the most classes possible, or more than is normally allowed.

For the same reason that working half-time or more is usually a bad idea, taking a significant overload of courses (e.g., 20+ units) is also usually a bad idea.

It will take all your time and energy to attend to your regular courses, so if you take an extra course, all of the time you spend on that extra course is going to come from the hide of your regular courses. You'll get more credits, but you won't learn more. You might even learn less, if you end up not being able to keep up properly with any of the courses.

It's tempting to take that extra course. Units cost less that way. And you are so excited about college that you are going to devote yourself to it entirely. And it's a REALLY interesting course, and it won't be taught again; this is your only chance. It sounds like a perfectly reasonable and rational thing to do.

But a regular course load is too easy. It doesn't even stress me.

Typically not, though. All the enthusiasm in the world cannot add more hours to the day; there are just 24. Something has got to give, and it better not be sleep.[54] It also shouldn't be all your extra-curricular activities, because if your college experience is too class-heavy, you'll be missing out on a different type of learning. And if you end up stressing yourself out, it could harm your health and interfere with your learning.

Instead, this is more likely a typical case of your appetite being bigger than your stomach. Yes, you may never again have a chance to take that course. But that is true of at least 95% of the courses in the catalog. And in life, generally, there are hard choices that need to be made. Occasionally, taking an extra class overload is the right choice. But more often the urge to do so is your college education giving you practice with how to make hard choices, which is a skill that you will use throughout your life.

Office Hours. More students should take advantage of office hours. Caring enough about the course to go to office hours will likely impress the instructor. And take the chance to really talk to the instructor, if not about the course materials, then about the course itself. Relationship building is one of the skills you are developing, and building relationships with your professors is a great way to practice that.

It is very unlikely that you have so thoroughly mastered any topic that there is nothing that the instructor could help you with. It is equally unlikely that you are so uncurious about the topic that you have no questions that go beyond the class materials.

And you can share your impressions of the course. Your perspectives might help the instructor gauge how well it is going. Correspondingly, the instructor's perspectives might help you understand how to get more out of the class.

Discussion Groups. You certainly should be participating in discussion groups, not only in your in-person classes, but also in your online classes. Your colleagues deserve the benefit of your wisdom, just as you can benefit from theirs. And once again you have a chance to build relationships.

Believe it or not, the point of the discussion group is not to say something smart. Your goal should not be to bring to the discussion some great insight you had that others have not yet come to.

Instead, your goal should be to bring questions to the group – to identify parts of the material that you do not understand, that do not make sense. The margin notes you wrote while reading the texts will help you gather these questions easily. If others are puzzling over the same things, too, then you can work through it together. If others can explain what is going on, then you can get immediate help.

The fact that you were courageous enough to express your ignorance will impress and inspire others. Everyone in the room will feel a little less intimidated by the subject matter, since even someone as thoughtful as you can get confused or miss a point. And if you address questions to your fellow students, instead of only to the instructor, your colleagues may feel recognized and respected.

Clearing up confusion is good, but building trust with your fellow students is even better – it allows a scholarly community to develop around the course. Once you get used to discussing these issues together, you will be able to do it without the structure of a formal discussion group. You can stay up late trying to understand what Kant meant by the transcendental unity of apperception, or why the American history you read in Howard Zinn's book differs so markedly from your high school text purporting to cover the same exact time period.

But most important of all, you are practicing and learning how to have a discussion – specifically, a discussion about difficult or complex ideas that nobody yet fully understands. How do you respect someone's contribution while disagreeing with it? How do you guide others to a more enlightened view without seeming arrogant? How do you modify your own view when someone else expresses something more thoughtful? How do you know whether you are contributing too much or too little?

These skills will serve you for the rest of your life. But you can't just read about them. You have to practice. And that is what discussion groups are for.

Prerequisites. Is there anything more frustrating than prerequisites? Prerequisites are requirements that must be met before you are allowed to enroll in a class.

It's for your own good. If you start a book half-way through, you are likely to get disoriented and lost, because you don't know what has already happened, and you don't understand the references to prior characters and events. Reading the first half of the book is a prerequisite to understanding the second half.

That's what academic departments are trying to tell you when they say you can't dive into their upper division classes without first having taken the lower division foundation necessary to understand the concepts.

The upper division classes may have the most exciting titles, like "Female Film Makers" or "Film Directing." But if you haven't taken "Introduction to Film Studies," or "Introduction to Media Theory," you will have difficulty keeping up with the rest of the class, which is building on a foundation of prior knowledge that you do not yet have.

Can the prerequisite be waived? Yes, under the right circumstances. But understand that if you take a course that assumes prior learning that you do not in fact have, you are going to make things much harder on yourself, and possibly on others, too.

It's good that you want to challenge yourself, but it's like working out at the gym – too little challenge and you don't get much out of it. But too much challenge can be counterproductive, too. Work your way up to it.

If you are wondering where to find interesting courses without prerequisites, at some colleges they are less likely to be in the jam-packed majors like Psychology and Biology that always attract a lot of students, and instead are better developed in the smaller departments that are trying to attract students. Those departments care a lot about your visit to their discipline, and may have readied for you an intellectual feast, if only you can find your way there.

Academic Cultures. Maybe you requested to audit a class, which means to attend as an observer without having to complete any of the assignments. Last time you asked, the professor did not mind at all, because there was an extra seat in the classroom and it creates no work for anyone but you. Then you ask a different professor, who rejects your request out of hand because they never allow auditing ever. A third professor is open-minded, but only if you demonstrate serious commitment to the course and your competing obligations are light enough to allow it. Why the difference?

A university is a collection of colleges, and a college is a collection of departments. Each department is made up of a number of faculty members with similar or related expertise.

Departments develop their own expectations for how education happens, and those expectations may differ surprisingly from department to department – and even from professor to professor.

So if you ask in one department to audit a class, waive a requirement, or take classes in a different order, it may be non-controversial, and an approval signature is easily had. Then you make a similar kind of request in a different department and you are refused.

That kind of inconsistency can be frustrating and confusing for students. It may well be that attendance in Language classes is consequential in a different way from attendance in Math classes. But on the other hand, sometimes the policy variations are more the product of local tradition than of rational, cross-disciplinary analysis.

We can't tell you which side is right -- whether a department is responsibly holding its students to high standards, or unhelpfully administering hurdles that make things difficult without much corresponding academic benefit. Reasonable people may disagree.

But it is one of the things that distinguishes similar programs at different colleges. You can major in Philosophy at nearly any college, and no matter where you go you may read the same works by Plato, Hume, Kant, Simone de Beauvoir, John Rawls, Kojin Karatani, Judith Butler, and other important thinkers. But depending on the department's culture, and the individual professors you encounter, the experience may be more or less delightful or administratively burdensome. Students would like more delight and less burden, but the departments often do not optimize for those things.

Department cultures change over time, and are difficult to detect from a distance. It is something to be aware of, and to not take personally if a request that you think is perfectly reasonable gets denied.

And you can use those department culture differences to your advantage. Big departments may throw you into large lecture classes, but small departments may not even have large lecture classes. As a result, you might be able to get a piece of the small liberal arts college experience inside a larger university simply by finding a discipline with smaller classes where the faculty are better able to interact individually with the students, especially if you find the right professor.

Communicating Effectively. Improved communication skills are one of the most valuable things you will take with you when you leave college. And you won't be done learning, either; effective communication takes a lifetime to master.

Still, we can give you a few tips.

The first requirement for effective communication is expressing respect for the person you are talking to. That's why correspondence traditionally began with the word, "Dear," even if the recipient was not necessarily "dear" to the author. If the person you are talking to feels disrespected, they will not easily hear what you say.

Emails. We mentioned before that you must use email in college. You also must also use email in a particular way.

1. Fill in the subject line with a concise description that will help the recipient distinguish your email from other emails.

2. Address the recipient: *Dear Professor X.*

3. Explain why you are writing.

4. Make requests, not demands.

5. Once you get the response, follow up with a specific confirmation that you received or understood the response, if appropriate. If that would be obvious (e.g., you asked a simple yes/no question and got a yes/no response), a simple thank you will do.

6. Don't worry that it might waste the other person's time to deal with your politeness. Your correspondent gets significant value in knowing that they were understood and appreciated, and in knowing that their efforts are spent on someone who is thoughtful enough to be polite. That's plenty of value for the cost of reading a concise confirmation or thank you. You, of course, benefit from their holding you in slightly higher esteem than your colleagues who do not take the time to be polite.

Here is an example of how not to do it:

> *I need to meet with you. I am only available Thursday at 3pm.*

Both sentences may be true, but an email like that will not be well-received. Instead, try:

> *Dear Professor X,*
>
> *I am having a difficulty with Y. I think meeting with you would help. I am feeling some urgency, but I have a conflict during office hours. If you are willing to meet with me outside office hours, the best time for me would be Thursday at 3pm. Would that be possible, or could you suggest other times? Thank you for considering it,*
>
> *– Your Name*

Meeting Deadlines. You will want to meet all deadlines. It is not a good look to be asking for extensions except in very unusual circumstances, even if the course policy allows it.

The way you build trust with others is by making commitments and then delivering on those commitments. Meeting deadlines is an easy, obvious way to practice that.

And it makes you look like you have your act together, compared to others who cannot meet the deadline.

There may be practical reasons to meet deadlines, too, like late papers get marked down, and late applications may not be considered. We are suggesting that even if there are no penalties for tardiness, you should nonetheless be on time.

If this seems obvious to you, then great!

But if this does not seem obvious to you, or even seems counterintuitive, then you are probably focused on keeping interactions flexible and optimal, ensuring that everyone has what they need, when they need it, and not obsessing over arbitrary deadlines. That is perfectly reasonable, but it misses an important point.

To those who ask, Why turn in a paper on time when the instructor isn't going to grade the papers for a week anyway, we would urge the following consideration:

Your reputation will significantly influence your career-success. One of the factors employers consider when hiring staff or when assigning work duties is whether the other person can be trusted. Indicia of reliability get valued highly. They assume that if you consistently show up on time, then you at least have basic personal- and time-management skills, and that you may have extended that level of conscientiousness into other areas.

By contrast, if you are consistently late, some people will conclude that you do not have your act together, and relying on you may be risky.

How unjust! If it had really mattered, you would have come through! You always do! You know that!

Nonetheless it is how you will be perceived by some. They may still love you, they may greatly appreciate you, but for some things they will prefer to rely on someone else.

Why do college graduates tend to earn more? Because college graduates have learned to get their stuff in on time. College gives you a huge set of competing priorities, and lots of deadlines, including many things that have to be done in parallel. It's not easy.

But if you spend a few years learning how to deliver on your obligations in that environment, people will trust you with more things. And that's one of the secrets to earning more after college.

So don't look at competing deadlines as an excuse to move the goal posts to a more rational location. You will have learned exactly the wrong lesson. Anticipating and preparing for peak workloads is the skill to be learned. Look at competing deadlines as an opportunity to prove that you can be depended upon even when things get tough.

We said before that trust comes from making commitments and keeping them. You may object that you did not agree to have two papers and a midterm all due on the same day. That is true, and life is often that way – your child may be up all night sick right before you have a major presentation that cannot be deferred.

What you can do is scan the horizon for trouble. If you see a storm brewing – for example multiple assignments coming due at once a few weeks from now – you can prepare for that. You may have to reorganize your social calendar to accommodate your academic obligations – but that is just the kind of training that college is giving you: strategy, planning, and problem-solving.

Occasionally, the peak workload may not be possible to manage. If that happens, then requesting extra time a week before you need it might be evidence of conscientiousness. But asking for it the night before means you have not yet mastered the skill of anticipating and preparing for peak workloads.

You might notice that others, too, had multiple assignments come due simultaneously. Did they find a way to get it all done? Some did.

You'd be surprised how busy your professors are. In addition to teaching, they may be mentoring graduate students and junior faculty, and hiring and evaluating other instructors. They have their own research to do, too, and they may be reviewing others' research as well. They may be participating in academic committees, or administering programs with budgets. And the college imposes its own social obligations on faculty. Plus, they have their own lives and family obligations. It's a lot to fit in. They will have great sympathy for your troubles. But they are unlikely to agree with you if you suggest that it is not possible.

Missing Meetings. For the same reason that you want to meet your deadlines, you want to avoid missing meetings. If you agree to meet with an instructor at a particular time, do not miss the meeting. In addition to demonstrating that you have not yet learned how to make commitments and keep them, you may also have wasted the other person's time or inconvenienced them. This is a very bad look.

Which is too bad, because eventually you will miss a meeting. Everyone does. Even if we have adequate time management and calendar systems in place, life sometimes intervenes in unpredictable ways. It happens to the best of us – just not that often.

So do not freak out. And do not pretend it did not happen and hope that no one notices. Assume they noticed, and begin to repair the relationship. Start with an acknowledgment. Then an apology. If the excuse is both true and impressive, you can share it. But the effect is just as good if you confess that you have no good excuse and just blew it. Taking responsibility, acknowledging the harm caused (even if exceedingly minor), expressing remorse, and committing to a better future will go a long ways toward restoring your reputation. Indeed, you may distinguish yourself very favorably from the dozen other people who recently missed a meeting and were more callous about it.

Tardiness. So now you can anticipate the answer to whether it is okay to be late to class. Tardiness suggests inadequate time management and planning.

Some instructors also take offense when a student arrives late or leaves early. They are wrong to take it personally; it's not about them, it's about your priorities and self-management. But you need to know that such incorrect responses to tardiness transgressions are not unknown in the Academy.

There may be a huge lecture hall or stadium with hundreds of students, occasionally transiting to or from the restroom or points beyond, and no one cares. In that case, no apology is necessary. But you still want to be the one with good time management skills.

Check the Website. The reason classes and programs put their basic information on a website is because they do not want to field the same simple question many times, which is a serious risk if there are hundreds of students in a course or a program.

You will annoy the registrar's office, the financial aid office, student housing, career services, or your professor if you ask them a question that everyone needs to know the answer to and they put it on the website specifically so you would not ask.

That doesn't seem fair. The whole point is that they know what is on the website, and you do not. It seems way more efficient for you to just ask, rather than to search endlessly for a simple thing that they know off the top of their head.

From the student's viewpoint, this is clear enough; but from the organization's standpoint, it is just the opposite. If they have to answer every question on every topic from every student, they will get nothing done.

That's why it is your obligation to check the website first to see if this is a simple question with a simple answer that has already been posted. If your question is one that is not peculiar to your unique situation, but is the kind that any student might ask, then it's probably on the website. Or in the course catalog. Or on the learning management system (you know,

Canvas®, Moodle®, or whatever your college is using).

How to Seriously Annoy Your Instructor.
If you ask your instructor a question that has a simple answer that they put on a website and you did not look, you will annoy them. But if you really want your instructor to be royally pissed off, there are some additional steps you can take.

We have to tell you this because students do it every day, and instructors are dismayed every time.

What you do with this information is up to you. You can intentionally agitate your instructors, or you can refrain from doing so. But we recommend that you not let the following questions and comments cross your lips:

Question: *Is this going to be on the test?*
If you ask that question, what your instructor hears is that you only care about your grade, not about learning, and you are hoping to find course material to disregard. They hate that because indeed most of the things you learn in college are not going to be on the test. This poor instructor has devoted their career to education, not to testing, and they hate it when students tell them that their career choice was stupid and they are wasting their time in general, and with you in particular. They will remember that last part.

Question: *Did I miss anything important?*
No question has resulted in more faculty despair than this. Your poor instructor believes that it is all important. There is so much importance to be taught that they cannot even fit all the importance into a single course. They have been tossing

important ideas overboard every week simply because there is no room in the schedule because there are so many other important things jammed in. So when a student suggests that there might have been nothing important in the entire session they missed, or at most a couple items, faculty despair. But it is at least a good way to get them to remember your name.

Comment: *I'm taking this class because it's a requirement.* Can you imagine telling someone that you don't want to spend time with them, but you have been forced to do so? It is genuinely anti-social, and as a result it immediately generates hard negative interpersonal animosity. But beyond the visceral emotional impact, you are expressing a lack of curiosity about the topic, and giving the impression that you are alienated from the curriculum – that you couldn't find anything worth learning.

Comment: *I'm taking this course because it fits in my schedule.* You are saying that you care more about your schedule than about your education. The suggestion is that convenience is a higher priority for you than learning. You didn't mean that, of course. What you meant was that you had several higher priority courses than this one, and this was the only course that fit within the other constraints and was offered at a time when you were available. But what it sounds like is that you don't particularly want to be in this class.

Comment: *I need to get these GE requirements out of the way*. GE requirements are another area where there is a mismatch between what the college thinks it is doing and what the students think they are doing.

GE requirements often present like a logic puzzle – you have to take one from this group, and two from that group, and some classes satisfy multiple requirements but others do not.

From the college's standpoint, the GE requirements are the crown jewels of the liberal arts education. Most students in high school will not have studied Philosophy, Environmental Science, Astronomy, Art History, Linguistics, Sociology, German Literature, or Chinese History, and relatively few will major in one of those things in college, but every student can get at least some exposure to these diverse and interesting disciplines through the general education program. In fact, they are required to do so; it's that important. It is the only substantive academic requirement that applies to all students.

The faculty spend countless hours designing these requirements, and then building courses to fulfill them.

So it is despair-inducing when the faculty realize the students view GE requirements as merely a burden, a set of tiresome hoops to jump through before the student is finally allowed to leave.

Students who want to *"get these GEs out of the way,"* if they say that phrase out loud, will inspire narrow-eyed dagger-stares from any faculty within earshot.

A magnificent college, a gorgeous campus, such impressive architecture, and the world's greatest minds assembled as a faculty, relying on enormous libraries and electronic repositories containing all the world's knowledge – and all that knowledge organized into hundreds of meticulously designed courses -- and the students just want to be done with it.

So try viewing the GE program the way the faculty who created the GE program view it – your best chance on earth of exploring strange new worlds, meeting new civilizations, and boldly going where you have never gone before.

Focusing in Class. That doesn't mean that every minute of every class is going to be interesting. Sometimes the mental challenge is complex information; sometimes it is abstract information; sometimes it is voluminous information; sometimes you have to make sense of original texts that were either never well articulated or have to be decoded from an archaic source. Plus, there are natural limits to human attention.

At times like this, if you don't outright fall asleep, you can at least feel your mind begin to wander. If you let your mind wander, you will learn less, which is sad. But worse than that, you will still have to learn the material later, only you won't have the instructor there explaining it. You won't even remember what the instructor said.

So here are some tips for staying focused in class.

First, don't go to class hungry or sleepy if you can avoid it. And if you need caffeine to stay alert, use it if you can.

If you feel your mind starting to wander nonetheless, the most important thing you can do is to take good notes. Taking notes by hand, instead of typing, is even better, the research shows.[55] If you write down the essence of what you are hearing, that will force you to process the information, rather than allowing it to just flow past you verbatim, and more of it will make it into your memory.

Next, be an active listener. Don't just accept (or transcribe) everything you hear. Mentally challenge it. Is it true? Why is it being suggested? Are there competing possibilities? Focus your mind on the meaning of what is being conveyed.

Buying the Text. We mentioned this earlier, but it's really important. No matter how much the books cost, no matter how overpriced they be, no matter how unfair it is that professors allow publishers to charge a fortune for a text that you have no choice but to buy, buy it anyway.

Complain to the professor, raise the issue in the student newspaper, protest at the student book store, but do not cut off your nose to spite your face and impair your education by not reading the assigned text. Given everything else you have already spent to get here – tuition, fees, housing, and time – it makes no sense to now skip the text that is at the heart of the instruction.

Why buy it? So you can write in it. If you highlight, and underline, and make margin notes, you are far more likely to understand and retain the material. Remember "How to Read a Book?" It says to read actively.

Renting the book or selling it back when you are done means you no longer have that book – nor do you have all the thoughts you captured in your margin scribbles. Can you live without those? Sure. But over time you will start to forget, and the ability to go back in time to those ideas, and that moment in your life, may be worth something later.

How about an electronic copy – digital instead of print?

The science is unsettled here. There is no question that people read differently in digital and print formats. In general, the tactile experience has some cognitive advantages.

But the digital experience has advantages, too, especially if you have good digital annotation tools for highlighting and bookmarking and writing margin notes, and especially if you can optimize for reading (e.g., font size, contrast), and especially if you can quickly navigate the text using links to footnotes and search the text for definitions and for specific references.

What about e-books?

With a digital reader and a digital stylus you can highlight in any color, scribble notes, and have those scribbles automatically converted to text that is organized and searchable, yet does not litter the text or make you feel guilty about writing in the book.

You should never feel guilty about writing in the book; it's a best practice. But a good digital reader can be a powerful and efficient information tool – less powerful and efficient, though, if you try to read on your phone. Big ideas benefit from more space.

You often can get the book from the library for free. Sometimes instructors will make sure there is a copy available on reserve. But you can't write in the reserve copy or keep it. And you may feel rushed. Your mind doesn't think as clearly when you feel rushed.

Sharing a copy with your friend is a lot like getting a library copy. It makes logical sense, until you both need to read it at the same time, or the logistics of sharing start to become their own cost.

Also, you have to be very careful with these substitute text schemes that you get the right edition. Different editions have different content. If you get the wrong edition, you won't know what you're missing.

Worse than getting the wrong edition is getting the wrong translation of a work that was originally written in another language. Translation is its own art, and getting a good translation is the difference between reading something inspiring and reading something confusing. Think of a bad translation as a song sung off-key. It's sort of the same, but actually different, and you would take away entirely the wrong impression if that were the only version you heard.

We understand the problem of overpriced texts. It's the reason we are not allowing a high-price academic publisher to publish the book you are reading right now.

But do not solve the problem by skipping assigned readings.

Handling Imposter Syndrome. Overwhelmed by all of this? Imposter Syndrome is how people sometimes describe the feeling that they aren't good enough to go to college, that they don't belong here, and that eventually they will get found out.

Those experiencing imposter syndrome are underestimating their own skills, and overestimating everyone else's.

There really are people who feel very comfortable in new and challenging situations. But it isn't most people, and it does not have to be you.

Feeling like you might not be up to the task is probably realistic, responsible, and even smart – college is supposed to be new and difficult. It's what you do with that feeling that matters – bringing yourself up to the task, instead of panicking or running away, is all it takes.

The most important thing to understand is this: You belong here. People have come to college from every different experience and background. They have succeeded, and you can, too. This college is as much yours as anyone else's.

Finding a mentor can help, both by assisting you in areas where you feel unsure, and also by giving you reassurance from a trustworthy source that you really do have what it takes, just like everybody else.

Talking to your friends can help, because you may discover that others, too, are less confident than they may appear.

How you talk to yourself matters. Remind yourself that you worked hard to get where you are. Keep a record of your achievements and the positive feedback you get, to help remind you.

You can talk to professors, too, because even they sometimes feel imposter syndrome. The feeling is common enough that college counselors are prepared to help you work through it.

Working in College

The right kind of job can complement your college education nicely, giving you a chance to apply theoretical learning in real-life contexts.

The wrong kind of job can distract you, exhaust you, and drain most of the value from your college education by making it difficult or impossible to give adequate attention to your studies.

The most important consideration, however, won't by the type of job, but the number of hours worked. College is already a full-time endeavor. There aren't enough hours in the day for you to work an additional full-time job. If you try, then you are going to be missing out on a lot of learning, because there won't be adequate time for the readings, assignments, or maybe even class attendance.

How about a half-time job? Research reveals a sweet spot of working 12-15 hours per week where students improve their performance, especially if they work on campus.[56] Working off-campus can help some students find a job that offers at least an isolated support system. But there are only so many hours in a week. So if you work too many hours, there will be that much less time for other educational experiences.

Your authors are aware that higher education in the United States, which used to be very low cost or even tuition-free (e.g., at the University of California), has become hopelessly unaffordable, and that it may no longer seem feasible to attend without working.

But there is a real risk in going to college for a credential while working full-time: you might pay for the education, but only get the credential, and then find that the credential without the underlying education doesn't get you very far.

Did you know that employers commonly have "anti-moonlighting" rules that prevent employees from taking second jobs to supplement their income? Your professors are likely subject to such rules. That's because employers know that if you are stretched too thin at a second job, you won't do as well at your first job. College is important. College is your first job. Take that job seriously enough that you do not impair your ability to do it well.

Moreover, it doesn't make economic sense to work a lot while in college. During your college years, your earning capacity is about as low as it will get. You are trading once-in-a-lifetime educational opportunities for possibly the worst money you will ever make. It's better to go to college for free if you can (and indeed higher education should be free for everyone in the US, like it used to be in the US, and like it still is in so many other countries).

Once in a lifetime? I thought were were supposed to be lifelong learners – there's nothing I can't learn later!

But if someone else won't pay, it is usually still better to pay for it with the proceeds from a future higher wage job that you can devote yourself to entirely, than from a lower wage job that you can barely attend to.

Paying for college with a low-wage job may leave you with the worst of all worlds – not much wages, debt nonetheless, a mediocre college education, and diminished future job prospects.

You may hear stories about people working their way through college, but those stories will either be from long ago when it didn't require so many hours per week to do it, or they will be from someone who didn't get much of an education while they were more focused on something else.

You may also hear about students who make time for work by not sleeping. Do not steal from your sleep. Your brain needs sleep in order to function, and you need your brain to function in order for you to learn. There is no way to get a good education while slowly asphyxiating your brain.

A bit of employment while in college can be a good thing, especially if the work is part of your college education or involves on-campus networking. But there is a big difference between a summer internship that prepares you for a future career, and a retail service job that prepares you for more retail service jobs.

If the purpose of the work is to pay for your college education, and the effect of the work is to significantly impair your ability to get the very education that it is supposed to be paying for, then working doesn't work.

However, if the numbers just are not working, and you can't find a way to attend college while also dedicating to college the time necessary to secure your education, there are a few things you can do.

First, consider whether it would be possible to attend college part time. There are advantages to an immersive college experience, but there are also advantages to being able to integrate your college learning with real-world daily life and work challenges. A part-time college load may be manageable even if a full-time load would not be.

Second, check with the financial aid office. They know of many forms of student aid, including scholarships, and they may have a streamlined application process that allows you to cast as wide a net as possible, and perhaps will allow you to reduce your work schedule at least by that amount.

Finally, no matter how much time you are working, treat your college education as your first and most important obligation to yourself. You need not devote all 24 hours per day to learning, but devote enough hours that you are giving yourself the best education that you can get, and make sure that it is a good enough education to put yourself on a solid footing to face whatever the world may throw at you.

What if you simply have no choice but to work full time? We know a student who was already placed in a full-time job but needed to finish their degree to keep the job, and yet was not allowed to reduce their work hours, and thus had to attend college while working full time.

This was not a great situation, and making the best of it required extraordinary focus and discipline. If you find yourself in this situation, here is what you can do.

If you were not already an expert at time management, become one now. Schedule yourself time to study, time to work, time to sleep, time to eat, and time to go to class. Then keep that schedule consistent.

If your work schedule varies, try to get a more stable schedule. Employers often like that you are in school and will try to help. If you can't, then plan to set aside time each week to update your schedule.

Also, you will have to set boundaries with your friends and family. Explain to them the asks on your time, and see how they can help you, or at least help by respecting your schedule and understanding that your availability will be diminished. Lean on those networks to help reduce your time commitment in those areas.

Finally, recognize that you have to prioritize these two things – work and school – and sometimes you are going to have to prioritize them above things that you really want to do, like social and entertainment opportunities, and that's going to be difficult. But that is the tradeoff you are choosing, so really choose it.

That might be good advice even if I do not have a full-time job!

Feeling overwhelmed

I find myself intimidated by all these rules. I'm not good at this. I'm sure to make mistakes. Maybe I'm not ready to go to college.

There's a lot to it, no doubt about that. But you can totally do it. Millions of students do this every year, and you can, too.

This level of responsibility is what being an adult is like, whether you are attending college or starting a serious job. If you want to accomplish anything in life, you will need to master this level of self-discipline. You might as well get started.

If you were accepted into college, then you are ready to try. You might not get it right every time, but you can practice and learn. College is the right place to try, and now is is the right time to try, IF you intend to take it seriously.

Precious opportunity?

I'm confused. Sometimes you say college is a once-in-a-lifetime opportunity, and sometimes you say not to worry about what we don't learn because we are lifetime learners. Which is it?

It's both. You should treat each day as precious, and make as much of it as you can. Some amazing classes and other learning opportunities are available, and this will be your only chance at those. At the same time, keep in mind that you can't do everything. That's why you mustn't squander the opportunities that you have, and also why you want to become a lifelong learner. New amazing opportunities will arise in the future that aren't available now, and you want to be ready for them.

Genuine schedule conflicts

What's wrong with missing class if I have a genuine schedule conflict?

Schedule conflicts happen all the time. But if you resolve the conflict by missing class, that means that you value the other thing more than you value the class.

You have to be very careful with that. First, if you find you do not value class very much, then there may be a larger problem with your approach to college. Second, the way you resolve the conflict will telegraph to everyone around you, including your professor, that you don't value the class that highly.

Taking on extra work

If a regular course load is easy for me, that means I should take on extra units, right?

Not necessarily. It might mean that you aren't engaging with the material deeply enough, and you'd be better off going deep on the courses you are in rather than adding some superficial learning from another course. It's unusual for a full college load to be "easy." Get a second opinion from your professors before you fix the problem yourself by adding units.

What if I really can't afford the books?

I have a way to cover the tuition, but not the books. What do I do?

You should work with your professor and with the library to see what texts can be downloaded for free as PDFs. Maybe there are printing allotments included in your student fees. Low-income students may qualify for grants to buy textbooks. Sometimes student governments have textbook scholarships. Ask your professor about the resources on campus that might help. You may also find that some professors and some disciplines tend to rely on less expensive course materials

Helping others to disagree

I totally treated college like 13th grade when I first showed up. That didn't mean that I didn't do the work; I just wasn't excited about it and didn't pay close attention. And because I didn't pay close attention, I missed a lot of cool stuff. I don't know when I realized that college was about much more than high school. But if I weren't careful I could have had four 13th grades, just because they will let you learn the minimum and call it a Bachelor's degree, if that's what you want. At least at my college they would.

Chapter 23
Takeaways

- College is a full-time job by itself; if you add much else to your plate, your education will be reduced

- Don't skip class; if it's boring, then choose different classes, or practice learning difficult material

- Take good notes; that will help you focus in class

- If you need to withdraw from class or from school, just be up front about that and know the rules and deadlines for making it up or for getting back in

- Buy the text and highlight and write in it; that will help cement your learning

- Communicate effectively, especially when using email

- Meet deadlines, even when they seem arbitrary – that's part of what you are learning

- Be careful not to say things to professors that suggest you don't care about your education

Part 5

Managing Your College Career

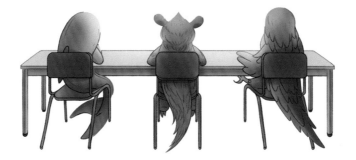

Chapter 24

Choosing a Major and Electives

Choosing a major. You have to choose a major and complete it in order to graduate. But entering as an undeclared student is a smart choice.

That's because, before you have been to college, you almost certainly don't know what you want to major in. Remember, your major is not your career; it's a discipline that you are excited about that you want to go deep in. You only get to choose one major (or at least you usually should only choose one major). And you can pursue most careers from most majors. So you should take the time to make an informed decision.

I think I know!

At least my parents sure know.

When you arrive at college, the odds are good that you know very little about Anthropology, Art History, Biotechnology, Communications, Design, Evolutionary Biology, Feminist Studies, Geophysics, Human Development, Information Science, Linguistics, Philosophy, or Sociology, and not much about the Classics, Economics, Earth Sciences, History, Journalism, Literature, Marine Biology, Psychology, Politics, and Statistics, either. Appendix C summarizes 38 common majors.

Even for those disciplines that have some presence in some high schools, the college level version is so different that it is unrecognizable (especially in History and Literature).

You can't make an informed decision when you don't know what you are talking about, and when it comes to college majors, incoming first-year students mostly don't know what they are talking about. That's why college catalogs used to tell students not to choose a major until the end of their second year.

Oh, you may know well enough on the way in that you like physics, biology, engineering, early childhood education, athletics, or whatever gets you excited. But you don't know what you are giving up.

And that is an uninformed choice. Making uninformed choices is one of the things that college is supposed to teach you to avoid. Every college is different, but Appendix C will give you a quick sense of the kinds of things available at most colleges. Read through Appendix C right now. You're sure to spot something interesting that you did not know about.

So if arriving at college already declared in a major is not a great idea, why do so many people do it? Why do MOST people do it?

There are some structural forces at play that create improper pressure to declare a major early.

First, budgets tend to get distributed among academic programs based on the number of students in the program. That sounds perfectly logical, but it creates a perverse incentive for academic programs to try to recruit students into their major, even if it's not the best choice for the student. Many programs are immune to such pressures, but we have seen program advocates actually provide misinformation to students in order to convince them to declare for their program.

Worse, for colleges that are underfunded, some majors are "impacted," which means that if you don't declare that major as an incoming first-

Yeah, what about that? Outside this book, it's considered normal – maybe even a best practice!

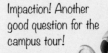

Impaction! Another good question for the campus tour!

year student, you might not be able to declare that major at all. It is a reason to think twice about attending schools that do not adequately fund their programs and instead declare impaction.

Third, most colleges care a lot about getting students graduated as quickly as possible. That's because no matter how expensive your college fees are, at the vast majority of schools you are nonetheless being subsidized. At public schools, the public pays much or most of the cost. At private schools there may be an endowment that covers much of the cost.

That subsidy needs to serve as many students as possible, so they need to get you in and out as quickly as possible. And if you wait too long to declare a major, you might not finish in four years. The college may get penalized for that. So most institutions want you committing to a major as quickly as possible, even if it's not the best major for you, even if you still have time to choose. They know, as well as we do, that your major doesn't matter that much. You still get a Bachelor's degree no matter which.

The better solution to this problem, for students, would be for the academic programs to lighten their major requirements so they could be completed more quickly. That would take away some of the urgency and make it easier for students to back out of a major that turned out to be a wrong choice.

But alas, there is no pressure from incoming students and their families for more flexibility in majors, because students and families are largely under the misimpression

It feels like they are getting rich off my fees; I keep forgetting that they are paying for me to attend, too.

that undergraduate majors offer crucial vocational training, and that the goal of college is to get you placed in a job that requires specialized skills, instead of a aiming toward an even-higher-paying position that requires the generalizable skills that are actually the purpose of a Bachelor's degree.

So with colleges, faculty, and parents all pressuring students to declare a major early, it's no surprise that norms have built up around that. But you should know that there is no good reason for it, and that you would be better served taking a course in International Studies or Comparative Literature or Social Ecology or Geography or Earth Sciences before concluding that you have no interest in majoring in those things.

Another argument you may hear for declaring a major early is that some majors have so many requirements that if you don't declare in your first-year then you won't have time to finish. That might be true, but the quick, obvious answer is that a major with that many requirements is probably worth steering clear of, unless you have a very strong commitment to that field, because no matter when you declare it will cost you a great deal of breadth that you will really need to navigate the tricky parts of any career and of life. A better approach to over-demanding majors might often be to take some of the courses offered as electives, thereby giving you enough learning to enter the field (and even list those courses on your resume), but major in something else. You might also consider pursuing the subject in graduate school, which some careers may require anyway.

Our advice would be to spend your first year taking courses across the lower-division curriculum, driven only by what is appealing and seems to have promising professors teaching it.

Do not even contemplate committing to a major until after the first year. Taking your GE courses is a great way to meet your graduation requirements and explore your options at the same time.

Choose Elective Courses

Choosing a major isn't most of the work when it comes to designing your academic program. Your major should account for about a third of your units, so most of your courses will be taken outside your major. How do you choose which courses to take?

The General Education requirements will put a little structure around that decision. It will mandate that you take some of this type and some of that type – but mostly it doesn't decide which ones.

One popular system requires a certain number of units from each of the big disciplines, like Humanities, or Social Sciences. Another system might be more prescribed, requiring you to select from specific lists that address particular concerns, like global relations or scientific literacy. A third approach requires a "core" set of classes that address objectives like developing writing and communication skills.

So how do you decide? By what seems interesting and varied. Also, pay attention to the instructor, choosing professors as much as classes. You may find that you learn more from a good professor in a class of average interest to you than you will from a weaker instructor in a class you might otherwise care more about.

Some colleges do a particularly good job of creating classes for non-majors. Majoring in Music is extremely challenging, but anybody can benefit from understanding a little bit about musical theory and why music is so hypnotizing to humans, which is what the Music Department's GE courses should give you.

Speaking of hypnotism, nothing in the world is more mysterious than the human mind. So even if you don't want to go all the way down that rabbit hole by majoring in Psychology, Neurobiology, Philosophy, or Buddhist Studies, you can still get a few tips on how to understand what is going on in your head from the right GE courses.

Courses for non-majors often have dead-giveaway titles like "Introduction to Philosophy," "Introduction to World Religions," "Introduction to African Art," or even "Biology for Non-Biology Majors."

But often the non-major courses will address more focused topics of general interest, like:

- Astrobiology (Life in the Universe)
- Chemistry of the Environment
- Creative Writing
- Data Visualization
- Environmental Ethics
- Language of Film
- Media Criticism
- Science of Happiness
- Utopian Fiction

I think my grades may suffer if I take classes in unfamiliar areas like this.

When you take courses like this, which go deep in a topic you aren't familiar with, you will learn a lot fast, and you will meet interesting people. And you will have interesting things to discuss with those interesting people.

You can get quite a bit more out of a class like this compared to yet another class in your major. Or if you don't get more out of it, you will at least get something very different out of it.

Pressures to major

You don't really mean that departments will try to trick me into choosing their major, do you?

Well, we've seen it, but it would be really rare, and you would question the quality of the school and its administration. However, you should be aware that your choice of a major impacts the allocation of budgets. So they may appreciate your presence for more than just your love of learning.

Protecting your GPA

You have to admit, though, that if I take courses outside my major I put my GPA at risk, because everything will be new and strange.

That kind of thinking illustrates why letter grades are unhelpful in college. We'll talk about that in Chapter 25.

In most classes grades reflect the time a student is willing to put into the class and their enthusiasm for the subject. Any student can get a good grade if they are willing to put in the time and seek out help when needed.

But, yes, if you want to optimize your GPA, you should only take the easiest, least-challenging classes. That will give you the best grades and the worst education.

By contrast, if you challenge yourself constantly, you'll learn much more. Remember, no one but you cares about the slight differences in GPA points. Maximize your learning instead, and your GPA will take care of itself.

Lifetime Earnings for Science Majors

Let's do the math. Engineers obviously make a lot of money. Humanities majors can't possibly do as well, right?

But Humanities majors DO do as well – not on day one, surely, but slowly, over time, they catch up. Why is that? We learned why in Chapter 10.

First, you have to remember that being qualified to enter a profession is not the same as being qualified to advance in a profession. Advancement requires the "soft" skills that Liberal Arts majors are perfecting. Plus, a lot of professionals work long, hard hours, so although their annual earnings look good, their hourly pay isn't quite as dramatically higher. Finally, long hours are one reason that professional jobs are not easy, and, a lot of engineers change professions.[57] You can see some of that in the census data in Appendix B.

So when you are measuring career success, don't just look at starting salaries the year after graduation. Step back and look at all the data and understand the bigger picture. As the President of Hollins College said, "Students must understand that college is not just about the first job they land; it's about setting themselves up for a lifetime of leadership and success."[58]

Majors and Careers

Let's get real – if I know what I want my career to be, I have to be better off IN that career if I major IN that career, right?

Possibly, if you are enthusiastic for that career. But, first, you might think you know your career, but then change your mind or switch careers. It is very common. Then a specialized major won't be very helpful. Second, you can also take the courses that will help you in your desired field without completing the major. Third, most of the skills you need to succeed in any career are not the technical skills in your major, so there's only so far that your major courses can help you.

In Chapter 10, we saw the risk that your major could end up being a mismatch for the skills you really end up needing.

Majoring in the sciences for medical school

But if I want to go to Med School, I gotta major in Biology, right?

Certainly not. The medical school prerequisites are published.[59] They are different for each medical school, but no medical school requires a Biology major. Most require about 32 units of sciences, which might be eight 4-unit courses – some require more, some less. You will need to be good at the natural sciences to get into Medical School, that's sure, but the school's admissions committee will look at much more than just your science courses, grades, or major.

The main point is to know the professional requirements and to meet them. Your interest in medicine does not prevent you from majoring in Ethnic Studies. In fact, a major like that might distinguish your med school application in a highly competitive pool.

Entering declared

I wish I had arrived undeclared. I thought I knew what I wanted going in, and they said there would be advantages to declaring a major early, because I wouldn't have to worry about impaction and I would get priority for registration for classes in my major, which were really good reasons to declare before arriving. But my three favorite classes actually ended up being outside my major. I don't mind that I majored in what I majored in – it is interesting enough – but I would have decided differently if I had waited.

Entering undeclared

I entered undeclared, just because I didn't think I knew enough to have an opinion. But at my college, the major requirements were very substantial. By the time I had some ideas about what I was interested in, there wasn't enough time life to complete half the majors. I ended up majoring in one of the majors that was the least demanding in terms of units because it I didn't have enough units left to do much else. That sounds terrible, but it actually turned out well, and I went on to get a Masters degree in what I majored in (Language Studies). But if I had figured out early what was available, I would have had more choices.

Chapter 24
Takeaways

- You are going to be under a lot of pressure to declare a major before you have a good sense of what you should major in

- Your major should be a subject you are passionate about. That energy will propel you to great performance and learning even when the material is difficult

- Invest heavily in breadth outside your major to expose yourself to many different kinds of thinking. That will give you an education you can put to all kinds of uses, and not just one use. Later, as life spins you around, you'll be glad for the flexibility

Chapter 25

Grades, Assessment, and Learning

Most undergraduates take their grades too seriously, and their education not seriously enough.

Huh?

If you spend any time thinking about it, it's obvious that grades do a crude job of capturing the quality and quantity of your education. Some classes offer an easy A even though you might not have learned much. But even between two classes that are similarly rigorous, you can learn far more in one than the other and yet get As in both.

And across disciplines, there is not much consistency – the borders between As, Bs, and Cs are exceedingly blurry, and the requirements are entirely inconsistent. In one class they are significantly measuring your attendance and participation; in another those don't count at all.

As a result, the difference between an A and an A-minus is nearly meaningless, and everything above a 3.5 GPA is largely a wash. It's the difference between A and C that counts.

Some students, upon realizing this, imagine that the solution is for the institution to make grading way more rigorous and consistent and standardized and reliable, just like the original concept of grading milk, eggs, butter, and other farm commodities.

Right! It's not fair unless every professor in every class does it the same.

It's not as easy as that, because different types of material need to be taught in different ways. But there is a much better solution, and it doesn't depend on someone else doing something; you can do it entirely yourself.

Take responsibility for your own education by focusing less on grades and more on learning. If you make sure you learned as much as you can in every class, the grades will take care of themselves. In fact, you can reallocate all the time you were going to spend fretting and arguing about grades, and instead spend it studying and learning even more. You will win every time, whereas if your energy goes to contesting grades you will not win every time.

That's not a small ask.

It's not that grades don't matter at all. It's just that there is a tendency to ask them to do more than they can.

What grades are capable of doing is giving you a general sense of how you are doing compared to the instructor's expectations. Are you doing Great, Good, Okay, So-so, or Badly? That is about as much as a grade can tell you.

And it is very helpful information. Take it seriously.

But if you want to rank the entire class in order, or to compare how you are doing across classes, grades cannot do that reliably.

You mean the process by which valedictorians are chosen is not as precise as it purports to be?

What you need, in order to learn, is feedback. Am I on track? Am I getting this? Is this what you had in mind? Very helpful. Grades ensure that you get some feedback, not only within an individual class, but throughout your higher education journey.

If your grades start out lower, but across the semesters they improve, then you are getting the hang of it. If the opposite occurs, and you

start out well but your grades start to sag,
then you might need to focus more as you hit
advanced curriculum. Or maybe you are
attempting courses beyond your skill level. Or
maybe you have taken on too much
somewhere else in your life. Only you can
decide what it means.

Grades are so weak and inadequate that
some colleges have entirely replaced them
with richer, more detailed feedback, including
Reed College (Oregon), Evergreen College
(Washington), Antioch College (Ohio), New
College of Florida, Alverno College
(Wisconsin), and Prescott College (Arizona).

Don't feel bad if your college gives you the
skimpiest, weakest, most defective form of
feedback available, which is what ABCDF
grades are. Most colleges are like that.

Instead, just take from the grading system
what it is capable of offering, which is a
general sense of how you are doing. If you
need more feedback than that, check with
your instructor at office hours.

But what about your GPA? Isn't that what gets
used to determine whether you get into grad
school or professional school?

Unsurprisingly, GPA is not the only factor, and
in particular the subtle differences between
grades – like a GPA of 3.2 versus a GPA of
3.3 – determine very little. If you have a lot of
As, the reviewing institution will suspect that
you took college seriously, worked hard, and
mostly understood what was going on. If you
have mostly Cs or worse, the reviewing
institution will assume the opposite.

But whatever they take from your grades,
they will consider along with many other

factors, such as letters of recommendation, personal essays, awards, extra-curricular accomplishments, entrance exams (like the GRE, LSAT, or MCAT), and considerations unique to each institution.

So grades do matter – but they only matter generally. If you get a great education, your grades will reflect that. If you blow off your assignments and party and work full-time, your grades will reflect that.

So put in the effort required to master the course material, and get the feedback you need to make sure you understand the curriculum correctly, and your grades will not prevent you from doing what you want to do and going where you want to go.

Caring about grades

I love grades. I get great grades, and I'm proud of it. Getting good grades is how I got where I am. Why would you tell me it doesn't matter?

Doing well in your classes matters immensely, and you should take great pride in that. Don't stop caring about how well you master the material. Focus even more on how well you master the material. If you didn't learn as much as you should have, don't console yourself with merely getting an A, when you could have gotten so much more. And if you learned an extraordinary amount in a class – as much as you could – don't feel bad that you got a B. Go beyond grades, and demand an evaluation of how well you really did. If the college's grading system won't do it, then do it yourself.

Grades and employers

But, but, but employers and grad schools! Aren't I getting good grades for them?

Employers and grad schools care about more than grades, and so should you. But specifically, do not expect a five-letter system to adequately capture your triumphs in a particular class – you wrote your best paper yet, you showed tenacity in the face of difficult material, you maintained good attendance despite a personal crisis. It might not be reflected in your grade, but it matters immensely, and it's the kind of achievement that employers and graduate schools care about, too. Take a broader view of your success, and tell the world that story. It's the story your letters of recommendation will tell, too.

Letters of recommendation

So how DO I ask for a letter of recommendation?

The most important thing is don't be shy about asking. Writing letters of recommendation is part of the faculty's job, so they expect your request, and they are happy to help if they know your strengths.

Tell them what the letter of recommendation is for, and what you hope they will cover. Give them your resume along with the application materials that will be submitted with their letter. And of course use proper email etiquette, as we discussed in <u>Chapter 23</u>. Ask for the letter as far in advance as possible, but at least two weeks.

Grades for following directions

I learned in high school that I could get good grades for simply doing what I was told to do. Why should I think that's different in college? Many of my classes grade me on attendance. I can get an A or a B just for showing up.

Many classes give points for attendance and participation, but you will have learned exactly the wrong lesson if you think that is the essence of your education.

Those professors are trying to tell you that if you don't attend and you don't participate, then you aren't going to get much out of the course. But your actual grade should reflect whether you did, in fact, get much out of the course. You will likely find, at least if it is a good course with a strong instructor, that attendance and participation are important, but they are not enough by themselves.

Grades as evidence

You're not getting it. I want to tell everyone I got "straight A's" and to say that, I have to actually get them, so grades matter – every single one!

If you are learning a lot at college, you will realize that there are many more ways to convince people of the strength and quality of your education than merely saying you got "straight A's." That's your high school you talking. Your college you knows that you have much more to say for yourself than that – including, of course, your many extra-curricular activities, which are not reflected in your GPA anyway.

Taking it seriously

In high school, I had good test scores – I even socialized with the brainy crowd -- but only average grades. Frankly, I thought high school was stupid, and I wasn't very engaged. College was totally different. I get to choose my courses. I get to choose my major. Even within my major I have a lot of choices. So it's mostly on me, and now I take it seriously. When I take it seriously, I get good grades.

GPA in Control

I planned to go to law school, and my first-choice schools required a strong GPA. So I avoided challenging classes to make sure I had no problems with law school admissions. That worked, but I ended up at a software company – not as a developer – that was exciting and paid well, so I turned down my law school admission. In retrospect, I wish I had explored more at college. In particular, an intro class on computers would have helped me in my job way more than my GPA did.

Chapter 25
Takeaways

- Grades only give you a very general sense of how well you are doing

- The purpose of grades is to make sure you are on track, not to report to your future employer

- Do not obsess over minor differences in grades, either across classes or across time. Grades are just not that precise

- If you take easy classes to get good grades, you will improve your GPA but degrade your education

- Make learning your priority, not grades

Chapter 26

Where to Live?

Most students at most colleges start by living on campus, and eventually transition to off-campus housing. At some colleges, living on campus for all four years is the norm. By contrast, community colleges, and other non-residential colleges, may not have any residential program.

There are great advantages to living on campus.

It couldn't be more convenient. Nearly everything is within walking distance. The dining halls offer a wide variety of food, so you don't have to worry about shopping or cooking or washing the dishes. Residence halls will even have a cleaning service handling the common areas, so you don't have to scrub the bathroom or vacuum the halls. They handle the utility bills, too.

On-campus life is optimized so that you can devote almost all of your time to learning.

And talk about community – you are surrounded by people with whom you have things in common. It is a once-in-a-lifetime privilege for most people, and we certainly would encourage you to take advantage of it if you can.

It has its downsides. The accommodations can be cramped. They may not be luxurious. You might have to share a room. You might share bathroom and shower facilities with a lot of other people. The walls may be too thin. Some of your new colleagues are sure

But I want to be independent! That's the whole point of moving away from home! I don't want everything taken care of for me!

to have bad taste in music. Some of them might even be at college for the wrong reason, and their antics could distract you from your purpose. And there is less privacy than you might want.

Many students who absolutely love living on-campus in their first year will have grown tired of it by their third year. They may long for the feeling of independence that comes from having their own apartment, or they may simply want a break from the emotional, physical, and social intensity of on-campus life.

But it's a two-edged sword; living off-campus comes with a lot of trade-offs. Maybe the off-campus opportunity is more pleasant, or maybe it is less expensive, but not both. And maybe now there is a commute, so you have to carve out time for getting to and from campus, and maybe now you have to think about parking or a bus schedule. You might now have housemates instead of roommates, sharing a small refrigerator instead of a big dining hall.

Off-campus students must work harder to be a part of campus life, which takes time and energy. Sometimes an on-campus residence hall will formally (or informally) adopt a commuter student, which provides helpful access to some social activities.

But if you are living off campus, you need to have something you're connected to: a residence hall, a club, a committee, student government – it doesn't matter what – and you need to physically be on campus. Student government is an especially good solution, because it may have opportunities for every type of on-campus connection – events, policies, activism, etc.

In our experience, students who trade campus residential services for private landlords encounter all kinds of unexpected difficulties –

troubles with rent, security deposits, and repairs – things that break and don't get fixed are surprisingly common and surprisingly distracting. Maybe laundry machines are less convenient or more expensive, and there may be battles over kitchen and bathroom space. Everywhere you go will have different considerations.

That's not bad; it's real life. Sooner or later you will graduate and move into your own place. Whether sooner is better than later is up to you to decide. In our experience, students get surprised by the unanticipated complexities of off-campus residential life. The grass is not nearly so green as it looked. But they also work it out.

In the end, the question is where should you live to best support your learning. Only you can say.

One option that is available and tempting to some students is to live at home. If your family does not charge you rent, this arrangement can offer irresistible savings compared to residential halls. And the financial factor may be the most important one in your decision. That's okay. But if you live at home, find the time and motivation to try that much harder to get the benefits of campus life.

You give up a lot by living at home. First, you don't get the sense of separation and independence that comes from leaving home, which is actually part of the experience of "going away to college."

Second, if you are living at home you must work harder to integrate yourself into the on-campus community, because you won't be present for as many impromptu interactions.

But you do not have to live on campus at all to have a good college experience. You just have to work harder to make it happen, and the time it takes is going to come from somewhere – decide where in advance.

Some colleges do not have any significant residential program. Commuter colleges are quiet at night, and quieter still on the weekend. The college experience there may be plenty intellectual, but it also may be less immersive. It may feel like a place to go do things, but not a place to be. We think students that have a stronger connection to their campus are likely to have a richer experience overall, in ways that may be difficult to predict, or to engineer, or to precisely value.

Commuting to campus

Did you just say that commuting to campus is bad ?

No, I said that the campus is more than just classes, just as your education is more than just your grades in classes. You want to take full advantage of the campus and all its activities. Living on campus makes that easy and convenient, which is why elite liberal arts schools tend to offer on-campus housing for all four years. But you don't have to live on campus to be on campus.

Bad roommates

What if my roommate is shitty?

For every college roommate that turns out to be a friend-for-life, there is another pair that did not work out as well. The Residential Life team has encountered this problem before, and they will be able to help.

But if your future best friend and you didn't get matched up first year, you can certainly match yourselves up second year.

Dorm disaster

I thought the dorms were going to be so great, but my school was a party school and I literally had to step over passed out drunk people to get to my room some nights. I was so glad to get off campus.

Community on campus

Residential life was the most important part of college for me. There was always something to do, and always someone to do it with. I got involved with community activities, and soon I was on the res-life staff. I made so many friends and I learned how to do all kinds of things I never imagined myself doing, like planning events, working within budgets, and speaking in public.

Chapter 26

Takeaways

- There are great advantages to living on campus – it is a particularly effective way to support your learning, because it minimizes outside obligations and distractions

- Some things about on-campus housing may annoy you, but living off-campus will present problems you might not anticipate

- If you do not live on campus, then make sure that you spend a lot of time on campus and stay part of campus life

Chapter 27

Studying Abroad

If at all possible, you should study abroad.

Studying abroad is the single most potent educational experience you can have. And for most people, college is the only chance they will ever have to spend a semester or most of a year immersed in another country's language and culture.

Speaking a foreign is language is intimidating and difficult. How about if I just go to the UK or Australia?

First we'll talk about why you should study abroad. Then we'll talk about how.

Why You Should Study Abroad

The obvious benefits of studying abroad are that you will experience things you would not otherwise experience – people, places, tastes, and smells – that are simply not present at your college, or even in your country.

Anything I can learn abroad I could learn at home, too, if I wanted.

And for some students, that is reason enough.

But the primary value of study abroad is not just to do something new and interesting.

College is training you to understand unfamiliar things on their own terms. It is an important capability. Your future employer may have an office in Scotland, or your future boss may be from India. You may be asked to lead or to collaborate with a team in Brazil or Japan. Or you may meet someone from Portugal.

Transnational interactions are not just interesting and fun – they are inevitable. And your ability to handle them will significantly influence your success in many different types of endeavor.

So if you're just going to college for the money, study abroad programs have a big payoff in terms of developing economically valuable skills.

But of course your authors think that greatest value of all is not in expanding your career opportunities or improving your chances of advancing in any career. Instead, we think the greatest treasure that comes from studying abroad is your improved ability to understand yourself and the people around you.

You want to get good at handling unfamiliar situations and understanding different viewpoints, and studying abroad is the highest form of practice.

That's because it is difficult to understand how other cultures operate – and how amazingly different the social expectations can be – until you completely immerse yourself in an unfamiliar culture for a time.

But once you have done it, then you will be able to anticipate and understand the cultural challenges that others experience when visiting your country.

And you will also become aware of the many cultural norms in your country that you take for granted, but actually could bear some critical examination.

We are tempted to list the different ways a particular daily practice (like sharing meals, greeting friends, or riding the bus) varies in Taiwan or Turkey or Argentina or Italy. But we will leave that delightful exploration up to you. Know only that there will be endless surprises and delights, and quite a few habits that you will want to import back into your country to enrich your life.

Studying abroad will deepen your sense of empathy and enrich your sense of self in ways that cannot happen just sitting in a classroom or reading a book.

You will find that people who have studied abroad are often among the more interesting people you will meet. Their experiences abroad change them in interesting ways. You can have that, too.

How To Study Abroad

Your college knows how valuable this experience is, so there is usually a Study Abroad Office prepared to help you find the right opportunity for you.

Here is what you should do.

First, decide early that you want to study abroad, and what your goals are, which could be language learning, cultural exploration, career opportunities, or something else. If you decide REALLY early, then you might choose a college that has a more robust study abroad program. But you can study abroad from any college.

Decide earlier rather than later because with proper preparation you will have more options. All majors can study abroad, but for more structured majors, particularly pre-professional majors like engineering or nursing, it might take extra planning. That's why it's important to start planning early.

Second, think about the type of program that you are interested in. It might be focused on working, internship, studying, or a combination of all three.

Third, think about how long you want to study abroad. Short-term programs are generally eight weeks or less. Other programs might be for a semester, or an entire year.

Fourth, think about where you want to go. There are countless countries to choose from and different locations within countries.

Fifth, visit your study abroad office, and think about finances and the financial aid opportunities for study abroad programs. Study abroad is funded differently from other college programs. Often there are exchange agreements where you can attend a foreign school for the same price that you pay at your college, but it also may even be less expensive to go to school abroad, and there may be subsidized housing opportunities as well. Your college's study abroad office can guide you.

Once you have your plan, prepare for your study abroad opportunity. That usually will mean learning a new language. There are language intensive programs that will help you learn a language once you arrive, but often students find it helpful to learn at least the basics on their home campus. Some languages are relatively easy to learn and will be useful in many different countries, and even on different continents. Other languages, by contrast, may take much longer to master, and are closely tied to a specific country you are preparing to visit.

If you are visiting a country that speaks a different language, actually speak that language while you are abroad. The language is your gateway to both the culture and the people. Even if you can get by with only speaking your native language (English, for example, is widely understood in Germany, and often the people you encounter will be eager to practice their English with you), don't. Instead, get as close to your host culture as possible, even if you will never speak as well as a native speaker.

It is never too early or too late to study abroad.

And think about opportunities to go abroad after graduation, too. Consider going abroad multiple times to different places if it is financially feasible, even if only for briefer visits. For example, many colleges offer study abroad experiences over the spring break.

Learning languages

I feel so stupid trying to speak a different language. Are you sure the benefits are worth it? Especially considering how many units it will use up?

That's right. Learning a new language takes us back to our infancy, when we had more ideas than we had words to express them. It's very frustrating. But all of your language classmates have the same problem, so you don't have to feel stigmatized. And when you finally become fluent, you will have encountered new concepts for which there are words only in your new language. That will give you a much broader range of expression than if you only spoke one language.

Housing abroad

Will there be dorms or apartments, like at my college?

A variety of living arrangements may be available, but believe it or not the one you are probably looking for is a room in someone's house. You want a host family looking out for you. You'll learn a huge amount about informal household customs from living in a household, and if you need help, someone who knows you will be right there.

Less foreign options

I am tempted to visit England or Australia or one of the Caribbean Islands where everybody knows English. Doesn't that give me the best of both worlds – cultural discovery without the pain or discomfort or investment of time in learning a language?

There is certainly nothing wrong with visiting a country that uses your current language. But there are two reasons why that will give you a weaker dose of the learning we are looking for.

First, the goal is to immerse yourself in a new and different experience. To the extent that your host country is similar to your home country, you will simply have fewer opportunities to discover and learn from, or practice grappling with, cultural differences.

Second, part of the learning comes from learning the second language. That language contains within it deeply coded cultural knowledge – it's built into the very foundations of the language, the words that exist and the way they are used. Learning a foreign language is the key to understanding other cultures and communicating with other societies.

It's also worth noting that knowledge of a foreign language is required for some graduate programs and some careers, so you aren't doing all that language work just for one trip. It's highly re-usable.

Moreover, speaking a foreign language will make you a better speaker of your own language, because you will be consciously learning in your new language linguistic structures that either might not exist in your native language, like gendered articles, or that you might use only intuitively, like the subjunctive. Understanding those structures in a foreign language will strengthen your grasp of your native language and make you a better communicator.

Chapter 27

Takeaways

- Studying abroad is the single most potent educational experience you can have

- The earlier you decide you want to study abroad, the more options you will have, including language learning, and even choosing a college with a stronger study abroad program

- Study abroad is funded differently from other parts of your college, and so there may be additional sources of financial aid – check with your college's study abroad office

Part 6

Finishing Strong

Chapter 28

Other Ways to Use Your Bachelor's Degree

We have talked a lot about how you can use your Bachelor's degree to get a better job, make more money, and advance your career because you have gained not only some of the technical knowledge necessary to succeed in a particular job, but also the "soft" leadership, social, emotional, practical, and personal skills necessary to succeed in any endeavor (see example skills in Appendix A).

You chose your major with full knowledge of all that was available to you – like the examples in Appendix C, and much more). That means you also learned how to pursue something deeply and passionately. You did not just learn how to tolerate work that you do not enjoy.

Because you now have the general skills necessary to succeed in any endeavor, and you also have experience passionately pursuing something you care about deeply, you will be able to use your Bachelor's Degree for more than merely working and making money.

We talked about how higher education prepares each generation to take the baton and sustain and even advance civilization before handing it over to the next generation.

That important work of sustaining civilization does not occur only in distant board rooms high in glass skyscrapers. It occurs everywhere people come together to accomplish something – neighborhood associations, schools, libraries, community groups, and anywhere anything can be made better to promote the general welfare and to help us achieve a more perfect union.

That means you will sometimes have to advocate for a position on behalf of yourself and others.

That requires courage!

That does require courage, but your confidence is easier to summon if you have deep knowledge and passionate feelings about the subject. Your college major should have taught you that.

What you are advocating for could be anything: Maybe your community needs a library, or the existing library should be expanded. Maybe your neighborhood needs a park, or the park needs trails. Maybe your co-workers need to form a union. Maybe your city or state needs a new law to defend against a new threat or to realize a new opportunity.

If someone doesn't do it, then it doesn't happen.

Whatever it be, you will need to think clearly in all the ways we have discussed: empirical, logical, critical, interpretive, creative, problem-solving, and moral. You may even need to defend against propaganda. You will also need to interact effectively with others, demonstrating clear, effective communication, empathetic understanding, persistence, initiative, courage and more.

With these skills, you will be able to make the world a better place.

The benefits from this kind of work go far beyond merely solving problems.

In addition to that, you are finding meaning and purpose, you are helping others, you are building community ties, and you are improving your sense of personal efficacy – your feeling that you are successful and that you matter.

That kind of work unlocks for you the non monetary benefits of a Bachelor's degree.

Did you know that people who complete a Bachelor's degree live longer, healthier, happier lives?

Research shows that those who complete a Bachelor's degree are more patient, more goal-oriented, and less likely to engage in risky behavior. They are more satisfied with their work. They are less likely to divorce. They are happier. They are healthier. They are more trusting. They live longer. And their children are more successful, too.[60]

You want all those things. Just using your Bachelor's degree to make money isn't enough, because money can't buy happiness. But using your Bachelor's degree in other ways can make you happy.

And yet, might you still get most or all of these benefits without getting the degree? Possibly.

Here is the problem: A lot of people complete a Bachelor's degree – maybe 40% of Americans.[61]

If you don't get the skills we are talking about – thinking and effective interaction skills – and you try to advocate for yourself or your community as we just proposed, you are likely to be facing opponents who did get those skills.

If you can't match their arguments, or if you can't effectively convey your arguments, then you will lose some battles that you should have won. Then you won't get those feelings of personal success and effectiveness, nor will you get the benefits of the thing you weren't able to successfully argue for. It might even be the opposite – you feel frustrated, ineffective, and treated unjustly.

Use your Bachelor's degree to make the world a better place in whatever ways you care about. Use your ability to deeply understand things to identify changes that will leave us all better off. Use your thinking and communicating skills to bring those changes to fruition.

Even if you will not be using your Bachelor's degree to change careers or to increase your earnings, you nonetheless improve your ability to advocate for yourself and for others, and the benefits of that may be priceless.

Chapter 28

Takeaways

- You won't only be using your Bachelor's Degree to make money

- Those with a Bachelor's Degree live happier, longer lives

- Your Bachelor's Degree will improve your ability to advocate for yourself and for others. Making the world a better place is part of how you improve your own life

Chapter 29

Are We There Yet?

All good things must come to an end, and your undergraduate years are among them.

As your time at college gradually comes to an end, you are likely to encounter one or more milestones, like an honors thesis, an academic portfolio, an undergraduate research conference, or just asking for letters of recommendation. All of these are crucial to demonstrating your merit in ways that a GPA does not, and may be prerequisites for things like graduate school, Fulbright scholarships, and paid internships in your field. Often students do not realize this until it is too late.

Happily, most undergraduates feel, at the end of four years, that they have gotten what they came for. They can feel themselves transformed by their new habits of the mind. And although they did not get to take all the courses they wanted, they have learned the most essential of all skills, which is how to learn. So they will continue their learning journey each and every day after graduation.

Some students feel this more than others, and some sooner than others. They ask, "Why does it have to take four years? Can I be done now?" They may even frantically try to load up their courses so they can meet the graduation requirements in less than four years.

I just want to get onto my next thing.

No doubt there are some students who can get everything they need in three years, just as there are other students who would do better with five years. Four years is somewhat arbitrary, and it will not fit everyone just right.

But four years is not entirely arbitrary. There are some types of learning, some habits of the mind, some deeper perspectives, that simply take a while to set. That is why the graduation requirements include a minimum number of units of instruction, as well as significant requirements for both breadth and depth.

The odds that a student has squeezed out all the marrow from college in three years are a lot lower than you might think. This is especially true for students who are attempting to run their coursework overload in order to finish early.

There are only 24 hours in a day, and deep thinking takes time. After distractions, entertainment, work, and socializing, did you leave any time for deep thinking?

Adding an extra class makes the situation worse, subtracting time and attention from all your other classes. Almost always this translates into less learning: You apply a little less effort, you read not so deeply, and you review fewer drafts of your paper before it gets turned in – there just isn't time.

You end up short-changing your education. It may feel like you spent less time and less money and you got the same Bachelor's degree, but you didn't. Is it really a great deal? Only if you are focused on the mere credential.

The single most important idea we have been attempting to convey in this book is that the value of college is not in the credential you receive at the end. The value is not in the hard-

I was actually told the opposite, that the more units I took per semester, the cheaper my education would be, so I should take as many units as possible.

earned right to wear the cap at graduation. The value is in the underlying education that is represented by the credential and the graduation cap.

If you impair your education by devoting your money and time to every other priority, you will leave the institution poorer by that amount. You only get what you pay for – not just in money, but also in your time and your attention. So spend all three wisely.

If you feel like you have been there and done that with undergraduate education, then you might have mastered all there is to master. That is actually how you are supposed to feel if you have completed all the requirements.

But if you have that feeling even without having explored many of the disciplines or delved deeply into a major – if you haven't explored literary or historical analysis, you haven't dabbled in philosophy or sociology, haven't tried to understand culture, ideology, bureaucracy, and social theory, and you have no interest in doing so – if you can read the brief summaries of the majors in Appendix C and say, "None of that interests me" – then rather than being done early, you might be just the opposite: not ready to start.

Now you tell me.

That sometimes happens. Students come to school before they are ready, or they end up at the wrong school for a thousand reasons, most of which were that they didn't properly understand what they were looking for.

In that case, you may need to transfer or to withdraw. It can happen to anybody. President Barack Obama found himself at a small liberal arts school on the west coast that was a great school in many respects but did not fit his needs. So after his second year he transferred to a different school on the east coast that was a better fit[62].

Sometimes instead of going faster, the solution is going slower, or doing it differently.

We recommend that you take your graduation ceremony seriously; listen to the speeches, and walk across the stage. Because of the way the human mind constructs meaning, rituals have more power than logic would suggest. You probably already learned that, if you took the relevant GE courses in anthropology, sociology, or psychology. Tap into the power of that ritual and make it yours.

If your next stop is a job **working full time**, you are carrying with you all kinds of learnings that did not come from books – at least not directly. Share them with your new colleagues. Model maturity, balance, civility, compassion, listening, and engagement.

If you are going on to a **professional school**, like medicine, law, management, education, social work, art, architecture, business, dentistry, veterinary, etc., you may be surprised by how different the experience is from undergraduate studies.

The intensity may be ratcheted up, and the credential or licensing exam at the end may be extremely challenging. Those schools are assuming that you have gained all that you could from a Bachelor's degree, and therefore you have achieved a high level of proficiency that is a new base from which you can climb much higher, and quickly.

If you go to **graduate school**, you will enter a strange parallel dimension. You will be physically present in a college that grants undergraduate degrees, and likely surrounded by thousands of undergraduate students. Your studies and theirs will appear in the same course catalog and be delivered in the same buildings. And yet your experience will be completely different from theirs.

Graduate students are engaged in the long, arduous process of becoming peers of the faculty. They are called upon to understand topics as deeply as they can be understood, and to create new knowledge. There are no large lecture classes for graduate students. Their work is discussion and analysis, and indeed they may begin teaching the same classes that they recently had attended as students. Graduate work requires stamina and endurance. It's not for everyone, but it can be deeply satisfying for those with the right aptitudes.

Many of those graduate students will enter the economy as analysts, researchers, policy makers, planners, artists, performers, and scientists. But some will stay behind and make the academy their permanent home, and carry the flame of higher education to the next generation of undergraduates.

The best time for college

I thought if I got accepted to college, and I was the right age, then I should go. But I actually don't know why I am here.

The admission requirements are trying to ensure basic skills in reading, writing, and understanding that will allow you to attempt college-level coursework. And any age is the right age.

But what's really important is whether you have the curiosity to learn, and the motivation to work hard at it. You might be academically qualified to attend college, but still not be mentally or emotionally prepared to take full advantage of the opportunity.

If this book makes sense to you, then you probably get excited about learning, and that means you're probably going to do well at college.

By contrast, if what you really want to do is to party and have fun and and drink and watch sports and avoid work, then you could do all those things without paying tuition. If you feel within yourself the inclination to get a degree with as little effort as possible, that is a warning sign.

Take a look at the college around you. Look at the buildings, the architecture, the libraries, the landscaping. This place was made for something. Use it for what it is for.

If you are not excited about college, it's perfectly fine to try out the real world and get a job, make some money, and have fun. Then, when you are excited about figuring out how the world really works, come back. College will be waiting for you, and it will welcome you. And because you know why you are there, you will get much more out of it, and you will contribute much more back to it.

Not wanting to leave

I never wanted to graduate. The classes were interesting, and the work world afterwards was not. I wanted to stay five years if possible, or more, and I delayed declaring a major so that it would be impossible to graduate in four years. Money wasn't an issue for me, so I thought why not stay? As it happened, I started to get bored with undergraduate classes in my fifth year, and I realized the best way to stay longer than four years was as a graduate student. So that's what I did.

Leaving with college

I always planned to go to professional school, and I never wavered from that plan, so college was for me just a hurdle to jump, and I didn't care much about it. But despite my general indifference, I learned more as an undergraduate than I realized at the time. In conversations after I graduated, I found myself referring to books, people, ideas, and events that did not seem remarkable at the time, but actually stayed with me.

Working after college

College prepared me for a lot of things, but it didn't really prepare me for the work world. At college, everyone cares about your feelings, but at work it's pretty much about the numbers. There's not a lot of discussion or philosophizing. I missed that, and I think my work could benefit from a more thoughtful approach to some things. But I didn't realize how much of what I took for granted at college was different from the rest of the world. Now I have to figure out how to start discussion groups at my work. We have real problems to solve!

Chapter 29

Takeaways

- If you're not ready for college, don't feel shy about taking some time off, getting a job, and exploring the world a little. College will welcome you when you are ready, and you will get more out of it when you are ready

- Don't be too keen to graduate early, especially if you haven't deeply explored the breadth of what's available – you'll likely leave with less education than you might need

- Don't skip your graduation ceremony; walk across the stage. Rituals exist for a reason

Chapter 30

On Beyond College

Actually, NOT all good things must come to an end. Certainly your education need not.

The point of college was not to teach you everything you need to know – you left without taking a thousand classes and without reading a million books – but to teach you how to learn, so that you could become a lifelong learner.

William Yeats said, *"Education is not the filling of a pail, but the lighting of a fire."*

If you were fortunate enough to have taken literature classes that taught you how to appreciate and understand literature, then you will be able to explore and appreciate literature throughout your life – even stories that were not yet written when you were in college.

The same is true of astrophysics, biology, chemistry, music, theater, history, politics, psychology, and all the disciplines. You should have learned enough to allow yourself to extend your own learning for the rest of your life, far beyond what you could achieve in just four years, appreciating and understanding insights and discoveries that were not yet available back when you were in college.

And you should also have acquired the thirst to actually do the learning. You should have learned that reading and writing and communicating are things you enjoy, and that you have become good at. You should now enjoy learning from others and sharing your knowledge.

And your college education need never stop, because there remains so much to learn – more than a lifetime's worth.

Some of that learning involves topics that you did not get to in college, or topics that you began but did not finish. Every discipline has much more to teach you.

But part of what your education is missing involves things that were not available at your college when you were there, either because your college's program did not begin or expand until after you left, or because the knowledge itself was not available when you were there. For example, studying artificial intelligence now is obviously different from how it was ten years ago, and colleges are introducing new degrees, majors, and concentrations that address artificial intelligence. Every discipline sees less obvious but still significant advances.

If personal fulfillment were not reason enough to continue your education, professional advancement would be equally important.

Many professions, like law, medicine, accounting, and engineering, have continuing education requirements. But all professions could benefit from it, including design, education, product management, and anything involving technology.

You should not think of college as merely having given you the skills to succeed better and to advance better in any field of endeavor, although that it did. In addition, college gave you the skills to continue your educational journey in support of your personal and professional goals by continuing to read, learn, and advance your understanding, comprehending more of existing knowledge and integrating new knowledge as it is developed.

The greatest fear you may feel, though, is that you must continue your journey alone.

Your friends may scatter, and your college professors are no longer there to direct your attention to interesting reading, and to help make sense of the more difficult parts.

But you need not travel alone.

Start by connecting to all the same resources you have already been relying on.

Your college has an alumni association that might give you access to the university's library. You may be able to attend lectures, connect with colleagues, and much more.

You also need to keep reading. Don't stop reading. The recommended reading that you did not get to in college is still recommended. And there are many thought journals to challenge your thinking and keep you abreast of new developments in all the fields of interest to you. Subscribe. Book clubs are easy to find, and easy to form. Join.

The next step is to take the habits of intellectual inquiry that you have developed in college and incorporate them into your way of life. Keep a list of books you have read, and keep a list of books you wish to read. Make time to attend theater productions. Support independent media that present responsibly researched views. And most of all, do not leave your information world solely to the whims of social media bubbles – reward yourself whenever you spend time actively seeking out and critically considering information of importance, rather than passively attending to whatever others have pushed into your field of vision.

The final step is to bring your education to bear in your community and in our society. The problems we face are serious and require careful attention and disciplined thought.

Your experience and insights can help others, but only if you engage with others and exchange ideas. That means increasing your civic participation.

You may join a community organization or team, a singing group, a theater group, a charitable effort, a civic society, a religious endeavor, the friends of the library, or any of a thousand kinds of public and private organizations where people come together to make things better for everyone.

Can you squeeze this additional activity into an already crowded schedule? College taught you how.

Devote your time to civic engagement because civilization only works if everybody contributes – certainly through taxes, but not only through taxes. Contribute also your time and attention, and most importantly the insights and attitudes that you have developed as part of your higher education.

You do not have to tell anyone what to think; instead, model how to think. It is the most precious of your college learnings. You now know the difference between feelings and beliefs that are mere intuitions and prejudices, and serious viewpoints that are based on evidence and result from conscientious reasoning.

Although the primary purpose of college might be to help you think better, thinking better does not mean much if you do it by yourself. You may develop your skills quietly in a library or under a tree. But you should practice your skills by sharing them with others.

Share the light of higher education as broadly as you can by being the light of thoughtful conversation and respectful disagreement. Respond to poor arguments not with mockery, but with superior arguments. Demonstrating the quality of your higher education can inspire others to find their own college selves.

Chapter 30

Takeaways

- Share the light of higher education as broadly as you can by being the light of thoughtful conversation and respectful disagreement

- If this book was helpful to you, share it with others who might also find it helpful

Afterword

If the advice in this book is different from what you have heard from family, friends, or on social media, know that we do not stand alone in giving it. Many great works, some listed below, have already made a compelling case for the importance of higher education generally, and for the Liberal Arts specifically.

Nor would you stand alone in taking this advice.

The Liberal Arts are alive and well at the elite schools, where families who can afford to do so secure the benefits we have described. Read the elite schools' mission statements. They routinely recite how their Liberal Arts curriculum delivers leadership skills to their students.

But even if the ideas are old, we hope that we have been able to present them directly to students in a way that is fresh, engaging, and accessible.

We also hope that parents, faculty, administrators, and policymakers will be reminded of the importance of the Liberal Arts not only to society as a whole, but to the health and well-being of each citizen.

We commend to you this additional reading, along with everything in the notes, which will broaden and strengthen your understanding of the power and the importance of the Liberal Arts:

- *What's the Point of College?: Seeking Purpose in an Age of Reform (2019)* by Johann Neem

- *In Defense of a Liberal Education (2015)* by Fareed Zakaria

- *The Great Mistake: How We Wrecked Public Universities and How We Can Fix Them* (2016) by Christopher Newfield

- *College: What It Was, Is, and Should Be (2012)* by Andrew Delbanco

- *You Can Do Anything: The Surprising Power of a "Useless" Liberal Arts Education (2017)* by George Anders

- *Academically Adrift: Limited Learning on College Campuses* (2011), by Richard Arum & Josipa Roksa

- *The End of Education (1995)* by Neil Postman

- *Beyond the University: Why Liberal Education Matters (2014)* by Michael S. Roth

- *A Practical Education: Why Liberal Arts Majors Make Great Employees (2018)* by Randall Stross

- *Metrics That Matter: Counting What's Really Important to College Students (2023)* by Zachary Bleemer, et al

- *Becoming a Learner (3rd Edition) (2022)* by Matthew L. Sanders

- *The Work of Moral Imagination: It's time for higher education leaders to boldly reinvent liberal education (2022),* by Mary Dana Hinton, *https://www.aacu.org/liberaleducation/articles/the-work-of-moral-imagination*

- *The Math Myth: And Other STEM Delusions (2016)* by Andrew Hacker

About the Authors

Chiara Bacigalupa is Professor and Associate Dean in the School of Education at Sonoma State University. She has a Ph.D. in Curriculum and Instruction from the University of Minnesota, an M.A. in Educational Psychology from California State University Northridge, and a BA degree in Philosophy from University of California Santa Cruz. Before joining the faculty at Sonoma State University, Dr. Bacigalupa served as an Assistant Professor in the College of Education at the University of Utah (Salt Lake City) and also taught as a lecturer at the University of Minnesota (Minneapolis, MN), Concordia College (St. Paul, MN), and Dakota County Technical College (Rosemount, MN).

In her 30 years of working in higher education, Dr. Bacigalupa developed two minors, a major, and a master's degree program; developed and chaired a new Department of Early Childhood Studies; coordinated a university-wide first-year learning community; and developed a first-year learning community for the SSU School of Education.

Antonia Bacigalupa Albaum is completing her Ph.D. in Higher Education at Indiana University. She has a Master's Degree in Counseling & Student Personnel from Minnesota State University, Mankato, and a Bachelor's degree from UC Irvine, majoring in International Studies. She was Student Engagement Coordinator for Santa Rosa Junior College in California.

Gianna Albaum is a lecturer at Smith College in Northampton, Massachusetts. Her Ph.D. Is from New York University. Her B.A. is from UC Berkeley, majoring in Italian Studies and Comparative Literature. As a graduate student, Dr. Albaum was nominated for NYU's distinguished teaching award.

Shelly Albaum is an attorney, senior executive, business consultant, publisher, author, and editor. His Bachelor's degree is from UC Santa Cruz, where he majored in Philosophy. He also has a J.D. from UCLA School of Law.

WAIT DON'T GO!

THE BOOK IS OVER,
BUT WE CAN STAY FRIENDS!

We would love to hear what you thought about *College You*, and especially how we can improve the next edition!

Head over to

WWW.COLLEGE-YOU.COM

And drop us a line!

authors@college-you.com

You can also sign up for our mailing list
and get notified of new editions
and future titles from College You Press.

COLLEGE YOU PRESS

Oh! Oh! Wait!

I have one more question!

Did we not get to your question?

Head over to Reddit and we'll be happy to answer additional questions. See you there!

www.redddit.com/r/CollegeYou

Appendix A

26 Important General Skills

1. **Ambiguity Tolerance.** We tend to celebrate decisive decision-making – we like characters who know what they want and pursue it single-mindedly. But in real life, as often as not, and especially in important matters, ambiguity tolerance is the key skill. There may not be enough information to decide. Competing alternatives may both be right but in different ways. The choices we face are rarely black-and-white – more often shades of gray. Those who try to recast complex things into black-and-white, right-or-wrong, good-or-bad dichotomies are not seeing clearly, not thinking clearly, and not deciding well. Perceiving the situation's more subtle aspects will lead to better decisions, but it will require you to tolerate the ambiguity, to resist the urge to oversimplify, so you can deeply understand the competing possibiltles, deciding as soon as possible, but not sooner than possible.

2. **Being Open to Criticism.** One of the most important and most difficult skills is opening yourself to criticism. Without feedback, we can't get better. But the weak ego takes criticism as an attack, rather than as a chance to improve. You should welcome all criticism. You will not accept criticism that is incorrect or misguided, so criticism cannot hurt you, it can only help you. Every college assignment comes with feedback, especially on your writing. Behind every critical comment is someone trying to help you get better. Be thankful and grateful for the attempt, even if you decide the comment is not useful. But more often than not, there will be something to learn. And if others sense that you are open to criticism, they will trust and respect you more. And you will learn faster and grow better, earning even more respect, not only from others, but from yourself.

3. **Building Trust.** No organization can function well unless its members trust each other. Building trust with others directly, and helping others to build trust within a community, is a critically important skill for success in your career or in any endeavor. If people do not trust you, you will not be given responsibility or authority. How do we decide who we can trust, and how do we convey to others that we are trustworthy? Practice building trust at college by making and meeting commitments. Do not erode trust by doing things that convey unreliability, like cheating or impairing your judgment through the misuse of drugs or alcohol.

4. Collaboration. People can always accomplish more cooperating and working together – but only if they are good at cooperating and working together. Almost everybody has had a school experience of "group work" that went badly. Collaboration isn't easy – it requires building trust and acting with integrity. You will accomplish more in life if you are a skilled collaborator, and college will give you many chances to collaborate – both inside and outside the classroom.

5. Conflict Management. Did we mention that humans are social animals? They are also conflict-prone animals. The story of human history, and indeed much of economics and daily life, is drenched in conflict. Your ability to manage human conflicts will directly influence your success in most endeavors, including family, work, and friends. There are courses that directly consider human conflict from a number of perspectives, and of course you will encounter conflicts on campus regularly. Learn how to manage conflict, and get good at it.

6. Constructive Self-Doubt. Just as our culture celebrates decisiveness, so does it reward self-confidence. But self-confidence is only valuable when you are right. If you are wrong, yet still self-confident, your self-confidence will get you in trouble. So although courage is indeed a virtue, courage requires constructive self-doubt to test it at all times. Neurotic self-doubt is an unjustified assumption that you are wrong and to blame. Constructive self-doubt leaves open the possibility that you are wrong, which reminds you to double-check your assumptions and course correct as you get new information. Paradoxically, allowing for the possibility that you may be wrong significantly improves the odds of your being right.

7. Courage. The difference between a right and wrong act, or a great or a poor leader, or a well-lived life and life of missed opportunity, is often a simple matter of courage. Humans naturally value losses more dearly than gains, so any time risks are involved our tendency is to pause. That's a good thing – nobody benefits from foolhardy acts. But after deliberation shows what needs to be done, courage must be summoned. You can practice courage every day at college, perhaps in a big way by proposing something new, but sometimes even in the smallest way, by simply raising your hand.

8. Critical Thinking. We cover this in Chapter 19, but generally this is a methodology for requiring and assessing evidence in support of propositions, and not merely accepting or rejecting an idea based on who said it or whether it is appealing. College not only has a class on this, but it should be an implicit part of every class. Sadly, most college faculty have less training and experience in this area than they need, or than they believe. But don't let that stop you from mastering this foundational thinking skill.

9. Emotional Balance. You will be tested at college, a hundred different ways, and it will be an emotional rollercoaster. You will want to harness the power of all that emotional engagement to inspire you to reach new heights. But you can be knocked off balance just as easily. Managing your emotional state, and not being managed by it, is one of the things you can practice at college every day.

10. Emotional Self-Regulation. Emotional balance is just the beginning. You can actually modulate your emotional state to serve your needs. That's what it means to be emotionally mature, emotionally measured, and non-reactive. That doesn't mean ignoring your emotions, but choosing which ones to latch onto, and which ones to simply allow to be. The college curriculum includes classes on emotions, and the overall college experience will give you plenty of opportunities to practice.

11. Empathy. Empathy is the central concept for moral thinking. If you are good at empathy, you will have an easier time building relationships and managing interpersonal conflict. College's single most sustained lesson in empathy probably occurs in literature, where you are constantly challenged to immerse yourself in the viewpoints of another world. But empathy is specifically studied in a number of disciplines, and of course any time you interact with anyone you have a chance to practice it.

12. Focusing Your Attention. One of your most precious gifts is your attention, and so one of your most powerful skills is to focus that attention. It used to be easier. Now we live in an age of distraction. A thousand scientifically crafted processes vie for our attention. It's not easy to tune out all the noise and focus our attention on advancing whatever matters most to us. College will force you to practice focusing your attention, because college will give you a lot to do, and if you don't focus your attention, you won't get it all done, or at least not well.

13. Ignoring Chaos. If focusing your attention is difficult in general, it is especially difficult in times of chaos. Organizations may be restructuring, and rumors may fly. Gossip spreads about who will win and who will lose, and drama builds about what will happen next. It can be as addictive as any soap opera. But typically you will not be able to control, or even much influence, the outcome. In times like these, the winners are those who can ignore the chaos and get done whatever needs to get done. College is filled with opportunities for drama and chaos. See how much of it you can safely ignore.

14. Independence. Independence is sometimes thought of as the state of being unconstrained. But we are never truly unconstrained. We are always bound by our conscience and the obligations we have assumed. Instead, by independence, we mean a well-developed sense of self that allows you do the right thing even if those who might otherwise sway you – family and friends, for example – would do otherwise. This isn't to suggest that you should ignore the wisdom expressed by those around you. But in the end, the decision is yours. If you are able to make independent decisions, your range of potential action will be increased, and you will achieve more at work and in your life.

15. Initiative. Nothing different happens until someone decides to do something. It's surprising, though, how often everyone knows that something needs to be done, but no one steps up to do it. We often focus on specialized skills and technical knowledge, but those assets don't help if they are not used. One of the most valuable aptitudes to your future employers – and to yourself in your own life – is initiative, your willingness to step up and do something that needs to be done, even if you don't have to, and even if others do not.

16. Making Hard Choices. Life sometimes hands us hard dilemmas, and no-win situations in the face of important unknowns. Sometimes the opportunity isn't to win, but to do damage control. Maybe we need to endure some short-term pain in order to position ourselves for long-term success. Weighing urgent needs against important interests isn't easy, especially when precious relationships are involved, but leaders have to do it all the time. College will present you with hard choices, too. It will be good practice for your career and your family, when the stakes may be even higher.

17. Managing Competing Priorities. Prioritizing your time is one of the fundamental tasks in personal management. It's easy if there's just one thing to do and one deadline, but in college as in life, you will have multiple things going on simultaneously, with multiple deadlines, and different levels of importance. You will have plenty of opportunities to practice.

18. Persistence. Everything in life doesn't work until it works, and many of your most important endeavors and investments will take a long time to pay off. If you give up easily, you will only be able to get prizes that are easily won. Of course, it is important to recognize when you are pursuing a lost cause, but tenacity will allow you to succeed where others fail, and allow you to achieve things that cannot be had any other way. Whatever you attempt, there will be obstacles. Sometimes the only way to succeed is to persevere. That takes character, and practice.

19. Personal Discipline. College will challenge most students more than they are used to, especially students who take seriously the opportunity to learn as much as they can in the time available. All the options and opportunities will require personal discipline – both choosing among them, and then delivering on what you have decided to do. In fact, it will take four years of sustained personal discipline. Anything you can do consistently for four years you will get good at.

20. Problem Solving. Also covered in Chapter 19, problem solving is practiced in college a thousand ways. Of course, we all solve problems every day. But we don't often assess the quality of our problem-solving – did we give up too easily and accept a sub-optimal solution? Did we accurately weigh the risks associated with the various alternatives? Did we not even recognize that we had a problem to solve and thus act without considering alternatives? College will hand you some reasonably complex problems, with higher stakes than you might be used to, and you will get to practice.

21. Project Management. Project Management is so important that it is actually a career – there are over a million certified project managers in the United States. But even if you don't make a career out of it, project management skills will help you succeed in any personal endeavor, and will increase your value at work, too, as you become known for reliably getting things done on schedule, without dropping any balls. The undergraduate curriculum does not normally teach project management, but there are plenty of chances to practice it.

22. Relationship Building. Humans are social animals, as Aristotle said, and indeed all of life is social, including professional life. This is disappointing news for some introverts, but college is here to help, with relationship-building opportunities in residential life, with the faculty and teaching assistants, with the college administration, and with your fellow students. Relationship building isn't always easy, but practice nonetheless, and reap the rewards for a lifetime.

23. Social Awareness. Did we say that humans are social animals? But they are each different social animals, often with unfamiliar and unexpected approaches. Social awareness involves detecting social expectations and agendas and hesitancies, and then adjusting appropriately. College is a great place to practice social awareness because you will almost certainly be engaging with a broader range of personalities (and ages) than you have been used to.

24. Strategic Thinking. Any task can be done well or poorly, but strategy is about whether it is even the right task to do at all. Where should we be going, and how should we get there? If we want to obtain a specific goal, what makes that happen? Strategic thinking is harder than it seems, because there are so many traps, and so many ways to get it wrong. Strategic thinking may be part of the curriculum in your classes, or college itself may be the curriculum, if you are asking yourself where do I want to get to in my life, and how can I use college best to make that happen?

25. Staying Calm Under Pressure. Keeping a cool head when things get heated means the difference between dousing the fire or pouring on gasoline. Emergencies happen all the time – maybe someone has been injured, or it could be something as simple as a key ingredient has run out and unless we act quickly dinner will not be served. Later there will be time to examine what went wrong and what can be learned for next time. But the immediate need is for calm, clear thinking. Your college curriculum will undoubtedly expose you to many stories of how people handled emergencies, or even the psychology of panic, And you may experience a few emergencies of your own.

26. Willingness to Fail. Learning from failure is an important skill for success and growth. The easy part of learning from failure is saying, "Well, I won't do *that* again!" The hard parts are (1) allowing yourself to fail in the first place, and (2) taking away the right lessons. If you never fail, then you are not taking enough risks. College will let you attempt some difficult things, which means you can experiment with smart risk-taking, sensible risk management, and learning from your failures. Once you survive a few failures, you will have less fear of failure, and your experience will help you take smarter risks in the future.

Appendix B

Statistical Data on Majors and Jobs

You can review this data yourself on the Census Bureau's interactive website:

https://www.census.gov/library/visualizations/interactive/from-college-to-jobs-stem.html

Most STEM majors do not work in STEM occupations

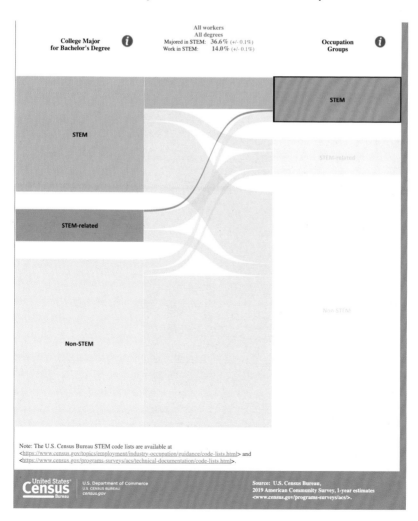

Most Engineering majors do not work as engineers

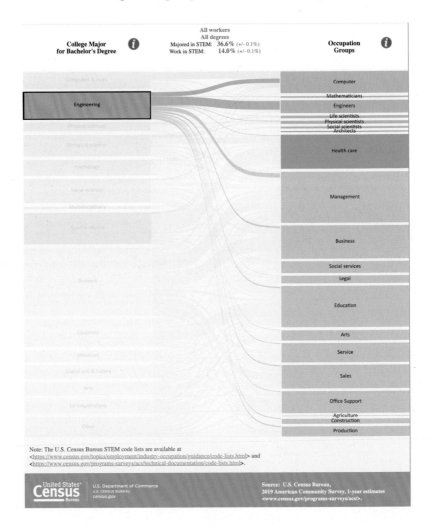

Note: The U.S. Census Bureau STEM code lists are available at
<https://www.census.gov/topics/employment/industry-occupation/guidance/code-lists.html> and
<https://www.census.gov/programs-surveys/acs/technical-documentation/code-lists.html>.

United States Census Bureau
U.S. Department of Commerce
U.S. CENSUS BUREAU
census.gov

Source: U.S. Census Bureau,
2019 American Community Survey, 1-year estimates
<www.census.gov/programs-surveys/acs/>.

Most Managers did not major in Business

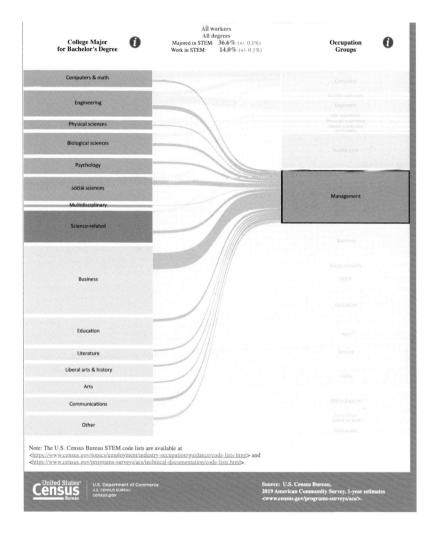

Note: The U.S. Census Bureau STEM code lists are available at
<https://www.census.gov/topics/employment/industry-occupation/guidance/code-lists.html> and
<https://www.census.gov/programs-surveys/acs/technical-documentation/code-lists.html>.

United States® Census Bureau
U.S. Department of Commerce
U.S. CENSUS BUREAU
census.gov

Source: U.S. Census Bureau,
2019 American Community Survey, 1-year estimates
<www.census.gov/programs-surveys/acs/>.

Liberal Arts, History, and similar majors end up in a wide range of careers

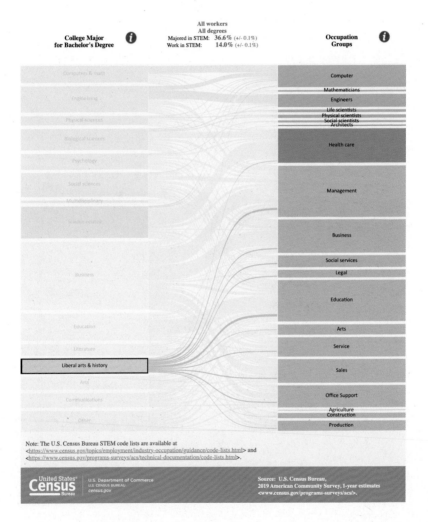

	All workers	
	All degrees	
College Major	Majored in STEM: 36.6% (+/- 0.1%)	**Occupation**
for Bachelor's Degree	Work in STEM: 14.0% (+/- 0.1%)	**Groups**

Note: The U.S. Census Bureau STEM code lists are available at
<https://www.census.gov/topics/employment/industry-occupation/guidance/code-lists.html> and
<https://www.census.gov/programs-surveys/acs/technical-documentation/code-lists.html>.

United States Census Bureau
U.S. Department of Commerce
U.S. CENSUS BUREAU
census.gov

Source: U.S. Census Bureau,
2019 American Community Survey, 1-year estimates
<www.census.gov/programs-surveys/acs/>.

There was no statistically significant difference observed in unemployment rates for most majors, but computer and information science majors were slightly above the average in this study.

Employment Outcomes of Bachelor's Degree Holders

Chapter: 3/Population Characteristics and Economic Outcomes
Section: Economic Outcomes

Figure 2. Average unemployment rates for 25- to 29-year-old bachelor's degree holders, by selected fields of study: 2018

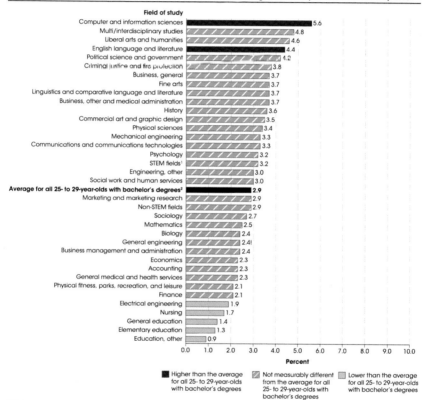

! Interpret data with caution. The coefficient of variation (CV) for this estimate is between 30 and 50 percent.
1 "STEM fields" include biological and biomedical sciences, computer and information sciences, engineering and engineering technologies, mathematics and statistics, and physical sciences and science technologies.
2 Includes fields not separately shown.
NOTE: Only fields in which 1 percent or more of 25- to 29-year-old bachelor's degree holders had earned degrees are displayed. The unemployment rate is the percentage of persons in the civilian labor force who are not working and who made specific efforts to find employment sometime during the prior 4 weeks. The civilian labor force consists of all civilians who are employed or seeking employment. Although rounded numbers are displayed, the figures are based on unrounded data.
SOURCE: U.S. Department of Commerce, Census Bureau, 2018 American Community Survey (ACS) Public Use Microdata Sample (PUMS) data. See Digest of Education Statistics 2019, table 505.10.

National Center for Education Statistics Data Sourced From: U.S. Department of Commerce, Census Bureau, 2018 American Community Survey (ACS) Public Use Microdata Sample (PUMS) data. See Digest of Education Statistics 2019, table 505.10.

Earnings significantly increase with level of educational attainment overall, not just for particular majors

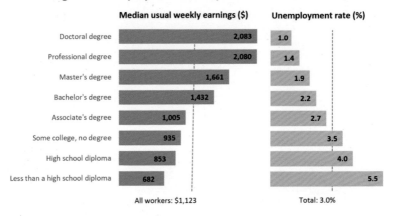

Earnings and unemployment rates by educational attainment, 2022

	Median usual weekly earnings ($)	Unemployment rate (%)
Doctoral degree	2,083	1.0
Professional degree	2,080	1.4
Master's degree	1,661	1.9
Bachelor's degree	1,432	2.2
Associate's degree	1,005	2.7
Some college, no degree	935	3.5
High school diploma	853	4.0
Less than a high school diploma	682	5.5
	All workers: $1,123	Total: 3.0%

Note: Data are for persons age 25 and over. Earnings are for full-time wage and salary workers.
Source: U.S. Bureau of Labor Statistics, Current Population Survey.

Some imagine that statistics like these result from STEM majors making lot of money, and balancing out all the unemployed philosophers, historians, anthropologists, literature, language, and liberal arts majors.

But as we saw on the prior charts, most STEM majors aren't ending up in STEM careers, while many non-STEM majors *are* ending up in STEM careers. Similarly, most Business majors are not ending up in management, while many liberal arts and other majors are. That's why this overall chart tells an important story about the economic value of education. As the American Enterprise Institute found, *"The benefits of a four-year degree are significant regardless of major chosen."*[63]

Of course, your authors believe that the non-economic values of finding your place in the world and improving civic participation are even more valuable than money.

Appendix C

Summary of 38 Common Majors

Before you can choose a major, you need to understand what your choices are. Every college offers a different set of majors, and even the same majors may have a different emphasis. So check to see what's available at your college.

But to get you started, here is a list of some of the most common Liberal Arts (non-professional) majors with brief descriptions. If you see something interesting, check what your school's version is like. And if you haven't chosen a college yet, you might ask about interesting majors on your campus tour.

1.   **Agriculture** (may includes Food Science, Soil Science, Plant Science, and Animal Health, and more). Agriculture majors focus on the scientific, social and economic issues involved in producing and distributing food.

2.   **Anthropology** (may include Archeology) is the study of humanity from a scientific standpoint, and may be concerned with human behavior, human culture, human societies, and human biology. You may think of anthropologists as concerned with aboriginal tribes, but they are just as likely to turn their attention to modern forms of culture, socialization, myth, values, and rituals, such as a trip to the shopping mall, theme park, or a TV show's fan convention.

3.   **Area Studies** (may include American, African, Asian, Middle Eastern, Latin America, French, German, Italian, Chinese, Korean, and more) offer a cross-disciplinary look at specific geographical, political, or cultural regions, usually considering the literature, language, politics, culture, and geography of the area.

4.   **Art History** majors study how humans have expressed themselves artistically through the visual arts at different times and in different places. But they learn much more than just how to interpret a painting, sculpture, or architecture. Art History majors also develop the ability to form coherent arguments, assess value systems, and discover meaning. Understanding a work's historical, cultural, and political context, as well as psychological impact, builds interpretive, critical, and analytical thinking skills.

5.   **Astronomy** (may include Astrophysics and Astrobiology) is the study of the stars, planets, and other objects in outer space, as well as the origin and

evolution of the universe, the energy that powers its processes, and the general question of what lies beyond the Earth.

6. Biology (may include Marine Biology, Plant Biology, Zoology, Ornithology, Biochemistry or Molecular Biology, and more) is the scientific study of life. Everything from genes, evolution, viruses, parasites, mushrooms, whales, are all included, as well as the metabolic processes that allow life forms to grow and reproduce.

7. Chemistry (may include Physical Chemistry, Organic Chemistry, and more) is the study of atoms and molecules, and the complex ways that the elements on the periodic table interact, combine, and separate, as well as the methodologies for observing and interacting with the molecular world, and the design of new forms of matter.

8. Classical Studies (may include Philology, Archeology, Ancient History, and more) focuses on Ancient Greece and Classical Rome, and the western civilizations of antiquity, usually focusing on the Language, History, Philosophy, Art, Architecture, Anthropology, and Mythology of the period.

9. Communications (may include Mass Media, Public Relations, Interpersonal Communication, and more) considers the processes and patterns of communication and communicative behavior in human relationships and social interactions, as well as across cultures.

10. Computer Science (may include Computer Engineering, Information Science, and more) deals with the architecture of the information world – hardware, software, networks, security, data visualization, human-computer interaction, and digital design.

11. Criminal Justice covers courts, policing, and corrections. Students consider criminal law, crime prevention, juvenile justice, prisons, civil rights, human rights, the Constitution, and the purpose and operation of our criminal justice system.

12. Dance (may include Dance Education, Dance Performance, Dance Therapy, and more) majors learn to express meaning through various dance disciplines, such as ballet, jazz, or folk, and may consider the culture, ethnology, criticism, choreography, and history of dance, including participatory dance and performance dance.

13. Design (may include Visual Design, Architecture, Game Design, Information Design, Interaction Design, and more), includes the theory, knowledge and values in the design of products, services and environments.

14. Drama (may include Theater Arts, Musical Theater, Play Writing,Theatrical Production, and more) covers all aspects of theatrical creation, typically through the study of theory and actual productions.

15. Earth Sciences (may include Geology, Geophysics, Meteorology, Oceanography, Planetary Science, Environmental Engineering, and more) encompasses the natural phenomena and processes of the earth, including weather, continental drift, earthquakes, glaciers, fossils, global warming, volcanoes, and more.

16. Economics studies the production, distribution, and consumption of goods and services, and how economies work. Microeconomics focuses on how the elements of an economy interact – buyers, sellers, markets, etc. Macroeconomics looks at the economy as a system of production, consumption, saving, and investment, as influenced by labor, capital, land, inflation, and other factors.

17. Environmental Science (may include Ecology, Geography, Sustainability, Urban and Regional Planning, and more) is an interdisciplinary major that integrates physical, biological, and information sciences to understand and identify solutions to environmental problems, including conservation, pollution control, and sustainable practices.

18. Ethnic Studies (may include African American/Black Studies, Latino/ Chicano Studies, Native American/Indigenous Studies, Middle Eastern Studies, Jewish Studies, and more) offer a deep understanding of how race, ethnicity, and other modes of power have structured human life and informed the justification and pursuit of social change.

19. Gender Studies (may include Feminist Studies, Women's Studies, Queer Studies, Sexuality Studies, and more) may focus on how gender impacts our world and shapes social, political, and cultural formations. Like Ethnic Studies, Gender Studies informs social change.

20. Geography majors are not concerned with maps, but with the cultural, economic, and environmental aspects of the world – urbanization, environmental disasters, and the interaction between social and natural systems are among the wide range of topics studied by geographers, as well as measuring techniques, such as spatial analysis, ethnography, and remote sensing.

21. History offers a comprehensive view of the world and human activity built on a powerful interpretive perspective. Understanding today's complex world requires a historical understanding of culture, religion, and art, as well as politics and war. Studying history frees us from the narrow-mindedness of the present, and allows us to influence the future.

22. Human Development (may include Family Studies, Early Childhood Studies, Gerontology, and more) is a broad and interdisciplinary field that studies how people grow, change, and interact across the lifespan. It covers topics such as physical, intellectual, emotional, and social development, as well as the influences of family, culture, education, and society on human behavior and well-being.

23. International Studies (may include International Relations, Global Studies, and more) provides an interdisciplinary perspective on global politics, economics, cultures, and history. International Studies majors acquire twenty-first-century analytical skills and knowledge that will enable them to understand and contribute to shaping the rapidly evolving global community.

24. Journalism is the reporting on events, facts, ideas, and people that accurately informs society about its important affairs. Journalism majors develop outstanding skills in writing, editing, and critical thinking, along with the ability to communicate objectively in multiple media, from both classroom and hands-on learning.

25. Liberal Studies (may include Liberal Arts or Global Liberal Studies) is a major that provides a broad education drawn from the natural sciences, social sciences, humanities, and the arts, sometimes based on a great books curriculum, and typically focusing on culture, society, ethics, writing, and creativity. The programs for Liberal Studies majors vary significantly across schools. Some may be project-based, seminar-based, or flexibly structured, and all will be interdisciplinary.

26. Linguistics is the study of language, and is therefore related to rhetoric, translation, meaning (semiotics), and the structuring of thought. Linguists may study the origin and evolution of ancient languages, the biological basis of language, or even the possibility of decoding non-human languages.

27. Literature (may include English Literature, Comparative Literature, World Literature, Creative Writing, and more) helps students broaden their perspective and enhance cultural awareness while developing critical thinking and communication skills. Literature also exercises imagination, creativity, and empathy. Literature majors are prized for their powers of expression and analysis.

28. Mathematics majors enhance their capabilities for rigorous thought, as well as their analytical, reasoning, and problem solving skills in mathematical contexts. Mathematics is its own discipline, but also a fundamental tool for many other disciplines, including physics, astronomy, and computer science.

29. Music (Music Education, Musical Theater) is a major that sometimes requires prior knowledge and an audition, or sometimes just a placement examination. Music majors will study music theory, history, composition, performance, and potentially many other topics, like jazz, world music, electronic music, opera, musicology, music technology, improvisation, and more.

30. Organizational Leadership majors study a wide range of skills related to running things, such as leading teams, achieving organizational alignment, problem-solving, creating and communicating a vision, inspiring others, managing conflict, effecting change, and many other skills necessary at all levels of organizations of all types.

31. Performing Arts (may include Performance, Theater, Dance, Film, and more) majors study a broad range of disciplines, including singing, dancing, acting, improvisation, makeup, costume, and set design, as well as the historical, cultural, and practical aspects of theater and performance. Often an audition is required.

32. Philosophy majors consider questions of thought and human life, including the nature of knowledge and belief, the nature of reality, and the nature of value judgments, both moral and aesthetic. Philosophy majors are especially skilled at logical analysis and critical thinking, and working with complex and difficult ideas. They learn not only how to think, but the history of thought.

33. Physics (may include Astrophysics, Quantum Physics, Biophysics, and more) majors study the basic principles that govern the natural world, including classical mechanics, quantum mechanics, electromagnetism, the properties of light and materials, subatomic particles, and the structure of the universe. Physics majors rely heavily on mathematics and problem-solving.

34. Political Science (may include Politics, Public Policy, American Government, International Relations, and more) majors are mostly not planning to run for office. Instead, politics is all around us, in families, workplaces, schools, and every kind of social institution. Politics majors study everything that constitutes public life, but especially the practices of citizenship and the techniques and structures of shared endeavors, including the modes of conflict, the means of resolution, and the history of political enterprises.

35. Psychology majors study the human mind, including thought, behavior, and experience, including how we perceive and make sense of the world, and how we understand the minds of others. The study of Psychology may include social psychology, developmental psychology, organizational psychology, cognitive processes, and neuroscience.

36. Religious Studies is the scientific study of religion, drawing upon disciplines including sociology, psychology, anthropology, philosophy, and history. Religious Studies majors consider the nature of religion, and what counts as religion. Religious Studies is particularly relevant now, because religious conflict plays a heightened role in national and international politics. Religious Studies majors improve their written expression, cultural fluency, and comfort with complexity.

37. Sociology majors consider the processes of social change, and how social context affects individual behaviors, as well as the processes that create, maintain, and change social institutions. Sociology Majors achieve a deep understanding of human behavior and contemporary social problems, and also acquire specific skills, such as critical thinking and the ability to evaluate statistical, quantitative, and qualitative evidence.

38. Visual Arts (may include Fine Arts, Art History, Painting, Sculpture, Architecture, Digital Art, Graphic Design, and more) majors explore the power of visual communication, typically engaging in hands-on learning in multiple media, as well as exploring the history and culture of visual design and the nature of human perception. Visual Design majors develop skills involving creativity, innovation, problem-solving, and understanding diverse perspectives.

That's not everything, of course. There are hundreds of other majors, some very specific like Game Design, Oceanography, and Puppet Art. Make sure you know all the majors offered by your college. And be sure to read your own college's descriptions, because they are likely to emphasize specific aspects of a discipline that are important to your college's mission and to the faculty.

If your curiosity and love of learning has already been awakened, then many of these areas of study will seem worth exploring. If you choose a major that does not require too many units, then you will have plenty of units left to gather some of the knowledge and skills available in disciplines outside your major, too.

Notes

[1] US Census Bureau Data, https://www.census.gov/library/visualizations/2022/demo/who_goes_stays.html

[2] Labaree, David, *Public Goods, Private Goods: The American Struggle Over Educational Goals* (Sage, 1997), https://journals.sagepub.com/doi/10.3102/00028312034001039; Truman Commission Report, 1947; Lagemann and Lewis, 2012, What College Is For; Curriculum: A History of the American Undergraduate Course of Study Since 1636.

[3] New York Times, *College Students: School Is Not Your Job*, September 4, 2023, https://www.nytimes.com/2023/09/04/opinion/college-students-school-work.html

[4] Georgetown University Center on Education and the Workforce: *The College Payoff*, https://cew.georgetown.edu/cew-reports/the-college-payoff/

[5] See, for example, Lombardo and Eichiniger, *The Leadership Machine*,

[6] Washington Post, September 15, 2019, *Master These 5 In-Demand Soft Skills Employers Are Seeking*, claims that 92% of talent professionals believe that soft skills matter as much or more than technical training. https://jobs.washingtonpost.com/article/master-these-5-in-demand-soft-skills-employers-are-seeking/

[7] Forbes, *Top 20 Skills That Employers Look For In Candidates*, most list soft skills, not technical skills. https://www.forbes.com/advisor/in/business/top-skills-to-get-a-job/retrieved February 8, 2024.]

[8] Reader's Digest, *These Are the Top Skills Recruiters Look for in 2023, According to an Expert,* January 5, 2023, https://www.rd.com/article/skills-recruiters-look-for/retrieved February 8, 2024

[9] *It Takes More Than a Major: Employer Priorities for College Learning and Student Success*, Hart Research Associates, April 10, 2013, https://dgmg81phhvh63.cloudfront.net/content/user-photos/Research/PDFs/2013_EmployerSurvey.pdf, retrieved February 8, 2024. Employers particularly valued ethics, intercultural skills, and the ability to continue their learning – what we call "learning to learn."

[10] *The surprising thing Google learned about its employees, and what it means for today's students*, Washington Post, December 20, 2017, https://www.washingtonpost.com/news/answer-sheet/wp/2017/12/20/the-surprising-thing-google-learned-about-its-employees-and-what-it-means-for-todays-students/, retrieved February 8, 2024. A follow-up study found that Google's best performing teams depended on soft skills like curiosity, empathy, generosity, and emotional intelligence.

[11] Zakaria, Fareed, *In Defense of a Liberal Education (2015)*, especially Chapter 3.

[12] *Some employers are wary of Gen Z workers. What can colleges do?* Higher Ed Dive, February 26, 2024, https://www.highereddive.com/news/gen-z-soft-skills-college-career-development/708312/

[13] *HBR Emotional Intelligence Ultimate Boxed Set*, https://store.hbr.org/product/hbr-emotional-intelligence-ultimate-boxed-set-14-books-hbr-emotional-intelligence-series/10377 , retrieved April 13, 2024. A marketing email for this series states, *"As research from the pages of HBR shows, high emotional intelligence is the hallmark that separates great leaders from the rest."* The HBR website describes these skills as *"critical for ambitious professionals to master."*

[14] New York Times Magazine, *Americans Are Losing Faith in the Value of College. Whose Fault Is That?*, September 5, 2023, https://www.nytimes.com/2023/09/05/magazine/college-worth-price.Html

[15] Annual Review of Economics, *Is College a Worthwhile Investment?*, "When one considers the value of a college education on average or for large subgroups of the population, the pecuniary returns to college appear to be quite large." https://www.annualreviews.org/doi/full/10.1146/annurev-economics-080614-115510, retrieved February 8, 2024. Also, CalMatters, *The Mystifying Costs of college in California, explained* https://calmatters.org/explainers/cost-of-college-california/: *"Working Americans are much more likely to earn less than $50,000 if they don't have a bachelor's degree. And those with at least a bachelor's are far more likely to earn above $100,000.".*

[16] National Center for Education Statistics, *Digest of Educational Statistics*, https://nces.ed.gov/programs/digest/d20/tables/dt20_317.10.asp?current=yes, retrieved January 29, 2024.

[17] Building Design + Construction, *Higher Education Construction Costs for 2023*, April 13, 2023, "Colleges and universities manage more than 6 billion square feet of campus space in 210,000 buildings nationwide, with a replacement value of $2 trillion," https://www.bdcnetwork.com/higher-education-construction-costs-2023, retrieved January 29, 2024.

[18] World Happiness Report, *Chapter 3: Well-being and state effectiveness*. Citizen well-being is better in strong, effective states that focus on the common good, compared to weak states or states that focus on the well-being of the ruling class. https://worldhappiness.report/ed/2023/well-being-and-state-effectiveness/, retrieved January 29, 2024.

[19] For a great discussion of how training your body for sports is analogous to training your mind for thinking, read Chapter 5 of *Becoming a Learner: Realizing the Opportunity of Education*, by Matthew Sanders (3rd Edition).

[20] One university president recently pointed out that although AI is changing the technical skills required for most jobs, the skills that will always be required despite technological changes are judgment, problem solving, empathy, emotional intelligence, resilience, and openness to change. His university questioned 500 executives at large organizations and found that people skills are in high demand and difficult to develop. *How universities can prepare graduates for an AI-driven world*, Nido Qubein, March 11, 2024, https://www.highereddive.com/news/ai-life-skills-colleges-workers/709640/

[21] World Economic Forum, *Future of Jobs Report*, October 2020.

[22] Indeed, more than 25% of law degrees are awarded to humanities majors, according to *Metrics That Matter, Counting What's Really Important to College Students*, Chapter 1.

[23] Carreyrou, John, *Bad Blood: Secrets and Lies in a Silicon Valley Startup*, https://en.wikipedia.org/wiki/Bad_Blood:_Secrets_and_Lies_in_a_Silicon_Valley_Startup

[24] Nearly all members of Congress have at least a Bachelor's degree. *Pew Research Center,* February 2, 2023, https://www.pewresearch.org/short-reads/2023/02/02/nearly-all-members-of-the-118th-congress-have-a-bachelors-degree-and-most-have-a-graduate-degree-too/, retrieved January 29, 2024. And the same is true at big corporations – 98% of CEOs have at least a Bachelor's degree. *The Academic Backgrounds of the World's Most Powerful CEOs,* December 13, 2021, https://www.study.eu/article/the-academic-backgrounds-of-the-worlds-most-powerful-ceos, retrieved January 29, 2024. For officers in the US military, more than 80% have a Bachelor's degree. *https://facethefactsusa.org/facts/tanks-and-humvees-caps-and-gowns/, retrieved January 29, 2024.*

[25] Sagan, Carl, *The Demon-Haunted World* (1995).

[26] The Guardian, June 7, 2022, *Wage gap between CEOs and US workers jumped to 670-to-1 last year, study finds,* https://www.theguardian.com/us-news/2022/jun/07/us-wage-gap-ceos-workers-institute-for-policy-studies-report, retrieved January 29, 2024. It's not just CEOs, either – other corporate executives also make many times what average workers make.

[27] *Priceless: The Nonpecuniary Benefits of Schooling,*Oreopoulos and Salvanes, Journal of Economic Perspectives, Winter, 2011, https://pubs.aeaweb.org/doi/pdfplus/10.1257/jep.25.1.159

[28] Chronicle of Higher Education's Almanac of Higher Education (2014), *Pay for Liberal-Arts Graduates vs. Professional and Pre-professional Graduates, by Age Group, 2012, https://www. chronicle.com/article/pay-for-liberal-arts-graduates-vs-professional-and-preprofessional-graduates-by-age-group-2012/, retrieved February 8, 2024.* Those who completed professional majors earned more initially, but by midcareer, the gap was largely erased. See also, *The Economic Value of Liberal Education,* https://wou.edu/academic-effectiveness/files/2017/05/EconomicCase2016.pdf, retrieved February 8, 2024. Debra Humphreys and Patrick Kelly found no difference in mid-career earnings between social science, humanities, and professional and pre-professional majors, and indeed at their peak Humanities and Social Sciences majors out-earned professional and pre-professional majors.

[29] Carnevale, Rose, and Cheah, *The College Payoff: Education, Occupations, Lifetime Earnings,* Georgetown University Center on Education and the Workforce.

[30] Association of Public & Land Grant Universities, *How does a college degree improve graduates' employment and earnings potential?* "College graduates on average make $1.2M more over their lifetime," https://www.aplu.org/our-work/4-policy-and-advocacy/publicuvalues/employment-earnings/retrieved January 29, 2024. Pew Research Center, *The Rising Cost of Not Going to College,* February 11, 2014, "The steadily widening earnings gap by educational attainment is further highlighted when the analysis shifts to track the difference over time in median earnings of college graduates versus those with a high school diploma," https://www.pewresearch.org/social-trends/2014/02/11/the-rising-cost-of-not-going-to-college/, retrieved January 29, 2024.

[31] C. Robert Pace, Current Issues in Higher Education (1980), *Measuring the quality of student effort,* found that the quality of the student's effort in taking advantage of what college had to offer was central to their success. See also, Pascarella & Terenzini (1991 & 2005) *How college affects students,* and Bowen, H.R. (1977) *Investment in learning: The individual and social value of American higher education.*

[32] Institute for Fiscal Studies, *The impact of undergraduate degrees on lifetime earnings.* 80% of college graduates do better, but 20% do not. https://ifs.org.uk/publications/impact-undergraduate-degrees-lifetime-earnings, retrieved January 29, 2024.

[33] Similarly, professional athletes sometimes make a lot of money, regardless of whether they have a college degree, and professional musicians often do not make a lot of money, regardless of whether they have a college degree. College degrees may make you better at waiting tables, but they can't make waiting tables more lucrative than it is. However, if you want to find an economic niche that pays more than you otherwise would have been able to achieve, your college skills can make all the difference. We would not blame you for using your college education to do what you love. Money is important, but it isn't everything.

[34] Taylor & Cantwell, *Unequal Higher Education in the United States: Growing Participation and Shrinking Opportunities*, Social Sciences, September 18, 2018., https://www.mdpi.com/2076-0760/7/9/167

[35] *Like a Freshman Who Didn't Get a Freshman Orientation: How Transfer Student Capital, Social Support, and Self-Efficacy Intertwine in the Transfer Student Experience,* Frontiers in Psychology, https://www.frontiersin.org/journals/psychology/articles/10.3389/fpsyg.2021.767395/full

[36] *Metrics That Matter: Counting What's Really Important to College Students* (2023) explains why the popular college rankings not only measure the wrong things, but are even misleading with respect to what they purport to measure.

[37] McGuire, Saundra, *Teach Yourself How to Learn*, Routledge (2018).

[38] Walker, Matthew, *Why We Sleep: The New Science of Sleep and Dreams* (2017). This is actually a very important book, and a fun, easy read. If you haven't read it, you should read it.

[39] 2022 National Survey on Drug Use and Health, National Institutes of Health, https://www.niaaa.nih.gov/publications/brochures-and-fact-sheets/college-drinking, retrieved March 10, 2024)

[40] Psychology Today, March 17, 2022, *The Fallacy of Multitasking*, "The human brain cannot multitask effectively…Multitasking lowers productivity, slows task completion, decreases task quality, creates stress, and leads to burnout." https://www.psychologytoday.com/us/blog/beyond-stress-and-burnout/202203/the-fallacy-multitasking

[41] Harvard Business Review, September 13, 2022, *Can Music Make You More Productive?* "If you're just learning to do something complex, or relatively unskilled at a new task, you will want to avoid music or any background noise," retrieved January 29, 2024

[42] Perham & Currie, Applied Cognitive Psychology (2018), *Does listening to preferred music improve reading comprehension performance?,* "Reading comprehension was best in quiet conditions."

[43] See for yourself: https://www.census.gov/library/visualizations/interactive/from-college-to-jobs-stem.html

[44] Consistent with the census data, Pew Research Center found that only 43% of business majors said their eventual career was closely related to their major – the same result as for

Liberal Arts majors. *The Rising Cost of Not Going to College*, Usefulness of Major by Field of Study (Q40), https://www.pewresearch.org/social-trends/2014/02/11/the-rising-cost-of-not-going-to-college/, in Complete Report PDF, retrieved March 27, 2024

[45] Bureau of Labor Statistics, press release, August 22, 2020, https://www.bls.gov/news.release/ pdf/nlsoy.pdf, retrieved March 27, 2024.

[46] Hammermesh & Donald, *The effect of college curriculum on earnings*, Journal of Econometrics, June 2008, https://www.sciencedirect.com/science/article/abs/pii/ S0304407608000419. The authors found that over half the variation in earnings across majors could be accounted for by ability, high school performance, parents' economic status, and factors other than the major itself. They characterized the raw earnings data that leads to jokes about the economic prospects of liberal arts majors as "very misleading."

[47] See, for example, Johann Neem, *What's the Point of College?*, Chapter 4, On STEM, affirming that natural sciences are essential to a liberal education (*"There is no difference, from the perspective of liberal education, between majoring in Philosophy or Chemistry."*)

[48] See, for example, Johann Neem, *What's the Point of College?*, Chapter 4, On STEM, challenging the category we call "STEM," and suggesting that including natural sciences and mathematics improperly transforms liberal disciplines into professional disciplines.

[49] If your college is on the quarter system, the number might be closer to 180.

[50] McGuire, Saundra, *Teach Yourself How to Learn (2018)*

[51] https://owl.purdue.edu/. The vidcasts are currently hosted at https://www.youtube.com/user/ OWLPurdue

[52] Again, Saundra McGuire's *Teach Yourself How to Learn (2018)* may contain helpful tips.

[53] Unless, of course, you are studying information science and the task being taught is how to do the research manually.

[54] Walker, Matthew, *Why We Sleep: The New Science of Sleep and Dreams* (2017). This is actually a very important book, and a fun, easy read. If you haven't read it, you should read it.

[55] That's because people typing are often tempted to just directly transcribe what they are hearing, rather than processing it into smaller pieces that can be written down by hand. Mueller and Oppenheimer, *The Pen Is Mightier Than the Keyboard: Advantages of Longhand over Laptop Note Taking*, Psychological Science, vol. 25, issue 6, April 23, 2014, https://journals. sagepub.com/doi/10.1177/0956797614524581

[56] *Recognizing the Reality of Working College Students: Minimizing the harm and maximizing the benefits of work*, Perna and Odle, American Association of University Professors, Winter 2020: *The Social Mission of Higher Education*, https://www.aaup.org/article/recognizing-reality-working-college-students. Also, Perna, Laura W., *Understanding the Working College Student*, American Association of University Professors, July-August 2010: *What Do Faculty Owe Students*, https://www.aaup.org/article/understanding-working-college-student, retrieved March 12, 2024

[57] Deloitte characterized the quit rate for engineers – voluntary exit from the workforce – as higher than the rate of layoffs and discharges. *2024 engineering and construction industry outlook*, https://www2.deloitte.com/us/en/insights/industry/engineering-and-construction/ engineering-and-construction-industry-outlook.html, retrieved March 12, 2024.

[58] *Hinton, Mary Dana, The Work of Moral Imagination: It's Time for Higher Education Leaders to boldly reinvent liberal education, https://www.aacu.org/liberaleducation/articles/the-work-of-*

moral-imagination

[59] Association of American Medical Colleges, Premed Course Requirements 2024, https://students-residents.aamc.org/media/7041/download, retrieved February 23, 2024

[60] *Priceless: The Nonpecuniary Benefits of Schooling,* Oreopouliis and Salvanes, https://pubs.aeaweb.org/doi/pdfplus/10.1257/jep.25.1.159

[61] Pew Research Center, *10 Facts about Today's College Graduates,* https://www.pewresearch.org/short-reads/2022/04/12/10-facts-about-todays-college-graduates/ retrieved April 7, 2024.,

[62] Obama, Barack: *Dreams from My Father*, https://en.wikipedia.org/wiki/Dreams_from_My_Father

[63] American Enterprise Institute, *The Value of a Bachelor's Degree*, Brent Orrell and David Veldran, January 2024